LET'S TALK
ABOUT GOD

*Devotions for Families
with Young Children*

by

GERTRUDE ANN PRIESTER

Illustrated by
R. O. FRY

THE WESTMINSTER PRESS
Philadelphia

Copyright © MCMLXVII The Westminster Press

Scripture quotations from the Revised Standard Version of the Bible are copyright, 1946 and 1952, by the Division of Christian Education of the National Council of Churches, and are used by permission.

LIBRARY OF CONGRESS CATALOG CARD No. 67–11494

Published by The Westminster Press®
Philadelphia, Pennsylvania

PRINTED IN THE UNITED STATES OF AMERICA

Contents

INTRODUCTION   9

I THE WORLD WE LIVE IN

Jamie and the Earthworms	15
Nothing from Nothing	17
How Old Are You?	20
" I Could Have Made It Better "	22
I Am Wonderfully Made!	25
God Saw that the World Was Good	28
The Day with No End	30
Old World — Or New?	33
I Hate the Dark!	36
The Magic of Tiny Things	38
Growing Up	40
Whose Dollar Is It?	43
God's Eyes	45
Darkness and Light	48
I Want to Go Home!	51
Is God Listening?	53
The Earth Is the Lord's	57

Make My Dog Get Better   59
What Is " Always "?   62
Don't Blame God   65

II GOD AND HIS PEOPLE

Who Is the Real Ruler?   71
Whom Do You Trust?   73
God's Strange Ways   76
The Biggest of All   79
" It Makes for Confidence "   82
God's Faithful Man   85
Who Makes the Rules?   88
The Ancient Paths   92
A God with Big Ears   94
Start Where You Are!   97
Love Is a Risk   100
God Doesn't Listen!   103
God's Surprises   106
God Is Always Ready   109
What Kind of Judge Is God?   111
Afraid to Go Home   112
Hello, God!   115
How Far Away Is " Lost "?   119

III CHRISTMASTIME

What Is a Holiday?   125
" I Wish "   127
Jesus Is a Special Person   131

Is Jesus a Real Person?   133

Our Neighbors Celebrate   136

IV   THE TEACHINGS OF JESUS

Two Mistakes   143

A Preacher Who Was Afraid   147

Road Signs   149

Gods for Sale   152

Wheat Versus Weeds   155

Are You Poor?   157

Over and Over Again   160

God's Forgiving Love   163

Do This! Don't Do That!   165

God's Ways — Or Man's Ways?   168

" I'll Pay Him Back! "   171

Someone Is Watching You!   174

That's Too Hard!   177

Let Your Light Shine   180

Ingroup or Outgroup?   183

The Puppet Show   185

" I Didn't See God! "   188

Real Friends   190

How Important Are Foundations?   194

Hold Your Tongue!   196

New Math in the Bible!   200

" Now I Can See! "   203

A Log and a Speck of Dust   206

V EASTER

Shouts of Praise . . . and Enemies
    Waiting!   212
Christ Is Risen Indeed!   215
Prove It!   218
Was It for Real?   221

VI HEROES OF THE FAITH

People with a Mind to Work   227
A Bishop and a Bandit   230
In the Name of Christ, Stop!   233
A Dangerous Book   235
Filled with Spirit!   238
Under a Haystack . . . but Not Fast
    Asleep!   241
Miss Tooter!   243

VII SPECIAL OCCASIONS

A Birthday   248
Give Us Courage, O God   251
Who Are You?   254
The Best Book of All   257
Beth's New Home   259
New Baby!   262
All Those Eyes!   264

SOME PRAYERS AND GRACES   267

SUPPLEMENTARY BOOKS   269

Introduction

" WHO WANTS TO TALK ABOUT GOD TODAY? " ASKED A CYN-ical friend. " No one has time anymore to include God in the family routine."

Regardless of whether or not we *want* to talk about God, God wants to be talked about. He wants people to wonder about him and to search out his ways. He wants his people to know him as their one true God who loves and cares for them, and whose power and mercy are still sufficient for the problems and fears created by the times in which we live. He wants us to worship him.

Children have a way of bringing up the subject of God when parents are least expecting it. Questions about him frequently have no quick and easy answer — indeed, they may have no answer at all! Yet such questions cannot be dismissed lightly. They often reveal deep-seated fears and misconceptions which parents must deal with, whether they want to talk about God just then or not.

In spite of what anyone may say, there are still many parents who want to make conversation about God and worship of him a natural and satisfying part of their family life. Some look back rather wistfully to customs of family devotions or Bible-reading and wish that they " could do something like that." Others have had no experience in their own childhood of any such devotional habits, but now sense a lack of " something religious " in their own family.

There is no one pattern or plan to follow in " talking about God " that will suit every family. Time is one of the biggest problems. To find a time when the whole family is together long enough to read and pray and talk together is almost impossible for many people. The wide span of interest and the extent of children's questions make it difficult to find any one collection of devotional materials that fills every need. The ability of parents to deal with certain questions but at the same time to be baffled by others calls for a wide variety of suggestions.

Therefore, the readings in this book are offered for your use in whatever way you find to be most effective in " talking about God " with your family. Perhaps you will find time as you sit together around the table at a daily meal to read and discuss some of them. There may be times when your children ask questions that are dealt with in one or more sections. You may wish to choose at random from the selections offered, to find the type to which your family responds best. Or you may try the " one a day " approach and work your way through the book, reading and discussing the ideas that are suggested to you.

Some families may find their children interested in reading parts of the book for themselves. Older boys and girls might like to take turns choosing selections to be used by the whole family. Some of the readings may lead you into a deeper study of one or another Bible passage as there is interest.

Bible-reading is uninteresting if the passages are too long or the words too difficult to read or understand. For this reason, the Scripture selections included here are generally very brief. Where a longer passage is indicated, it is hoped that parents will choose verses to read and will fill in between with their own sense of the meaning. Verses are sometimes quoted, but as often are stated in simple words by the author. It is hoped that you will have a copy of the Revised Standard Version of the Bible from which to read. In addition, it will be much more interesting if you can read from one of the translations in modern English, to find the freshness of old words in present-day language. The section " Supplementary Books " includes suggestions of such translations.

> I will give thanks to the Lord with my whole
>   heart;
> I will tell of all thy wonderful deeds.
> I will be glad and exhult in thee,
>   I will sing praises to thy name, O Most
>   High.
>
> (Psalm 9:1-2.)

The World We Live In

I

THE EXCITEMENT AND THE WONDER OVER the exploits of man in outer space bring with them a whole new set of questions and fears about what may happen to us and our world. Children as well as adults worry about what man may find " out there " that will upset all that we think we know about the way in which our world operates. People are asking more questions than ever about who made the world. Those who believe that God is the creator of the universe are taking a long look at what they have always believed, to see whether or not it will stand in the light of new scientific discoveries. There is a strange fear abroad that perhaps man is on the verge of " catching up with God."

Children know far more about the world than most of their parents did when they were their age. Parents should know far more about God than their children do, because they have had longer to know him and learn about his way. Children and parents together can therefore search for answers and assurance about their questions and fears regarding the world and its orderliness.

As Christians, we believe that God *is* the ruler of his universe. We believe that in Jesus Christ he proved his power over the strongest force of all — even death itself. Why, then, should we fear that because man has pushed out the boundaries of the known world, God may be found unequal to the task of ruling *that* part of his universe which man has been so long in discovering?

Likewise, we believe that God has a plan for his world, and that there is a basic orderliness to it that cannot be destroyed. Why do we try to blame God for man's careless use of the world's riches, and make God responsible for the troubles that come upon man as the result of his own selfish actions? Why must we have everything turn out the way *we* think is " right " and " good " in order to believe that God's plan is still in operation?

The following readings may help to raise as well as to

answer some of these questions. There are no easy and complete explanations for you to hand on to children when they bring to you their fears and questions, but perhaps there are guides to some ways by which you can find in God's word and through his mighty acts the reassurance that he will continue in our time to keep the promises that he made long ago to his people — to love them and care for them. In return he continues to expect our trust and obedience to his way, and our faithfulness in following the way of love that Jesus teaches us.

Jamie and the Earthworms

IT WAS A DAY WHEN LITTLE GREEN SHOOTS HAD SUDDENLY appeared in the garden space beside the back door. It was a day when the sun felt so good and warm that a boy just *had* to take off his sweater. It was a day when you knew that spring was really here! And it was a day when Jamie decided to take care of the earthworms.

First he collected his favorite wooden blocks that Mother had bought from the man at the lumberyard. These were long and straight, and Jamie had built houses and garages and boat docks with them all winter long. Now he took them outside where the sun was shining on the warm, black earth beside the porch steps. There he carefully set up one block,

then another, and another until he had closed in a narrow strip of dirt.

"Now it needs a roof," said Jamie, "because the sun is very hot."

After a while he came back with a long, thin board. "There! That's the roof," he said, laying it on top of the wooden blocks. He leaned way down to look inside the cool, dark tunnel. "Just the way earthworms like it," said Jamie.

Now to find the earthworms. Jamie carefully turned over the earth until he found something wiggling here and wiggling there. He picked up the wiggly worms and put them inside the house that he had made for them. When he had collected all the worms that he could find, Jamie sat back and hummed a little tune — one he liked to hum when he had done something that made him feel good inside.

Mother came to the doorway and listened to the humming. She saw the long, narrow house in the earth beside the porch. She saw the smile on Jamie's face.

"I've been taking care of the earthworms," said Jamie. "I made a house for them with my blocks. Then I dug them up and moved them in. It was too hot for them in the sun. They like it cool and dark."

Mother smiled. "You're all hot and dirty, Jamie. You must have worked hard for your earthworms."

Jamie nodded his head up and down three times. "I did work hard, for a long time, too. I'm hungry now. But you know, Mother, you don't mind looking after something you really care about!"

Mother sat down on the steps. "You're right as right can be," she said. "And that is part of God's plan for his world and all his people. He knows that people who love each other don't mind working hard to take care of one another."

"You and Daddy work hard taking care of me," said Jamie. "And you take care of Ann too."

"That's right," said Mother, "because we love you both very much."

" Even when you get tired and have a headache," said Jamie, sitting down close beside his mother.

" Yes, even then," said Mother.

" Does God ever get tired and have headaches? " Jamie asked.

Mother thought for a minute. " I'm sure God feels very bad about it when his people do not love each other, and when he knows they are not helping those who need their help and care. That must make God feel much worse than I do with my headaches. But nothing will ever make God stop loving us, Jamie. It's just as you said — even when it is hard work, you don't mind looking after someone you really care about."

"I'm hungry," said Jamie. " Let's get some lunch. I'm glad God planned for people to be taken care of — and my earthworms too."

A PRAYER / *Thank you, God, for your love and care. Thank you that Jesus came to show us that nothing will ever make you stop loving us, even when we do wrong. Help us to love you by showing love and caring for others. Amen.*

Nothing from Nothing

IF YOU SAW THE PLAY OR THE MOVIE " THE SOUND OF Music," you may remember the song that Maria sings when she is thinking about all the love and happiness that have come into her life. Where does it all come from? How did it happen to me? As she puzzles over questions like these, she decides that " nothing comes from *nothing!* " Love and kindness and beauty must come from someone or somewhere. They don't come from simply nothing!

There are some songs in the Bible in the book of The Psalms that sound as though the Hebrew people of long ago must have puzzled over some of these same things. They watched the stars in the night sky, saw them move about in an orderly way, and they counted the four phases of the moon that never failed to grow large and small and large again. They awoke to find the sun rising every morning in the east, and they learned that it would always set in the west. They saw the high mountains that stood strong and immovable even when the worst storms and winds blew around them. They watched their animals give birth to little ones. They saw their own families grow. They knew that the world was full of great and wonderful things that they could not understand. But they also knew that these great and wonderful things did not happen by accident. They came from somewhere, from someone — not from nothing. They came from God.

Today we still sing the songs these ancient people sang. Sometimes we read the words instead of singing them. You can read some of them in Psalm 19:1-3.

> " The heavens are telling the glory of God;
>   and the firmament proclaims his handiwork.
> Day to day pours forth speech,
>   and night to night declares knowledge."

The Hebrews who lived long, long ago were learning about the one God, who in his power and might and love had promised to care for them and make them a great people. As they learned more about the world in which they lived, they knew that only the one great God could be the creator of such a world. They puzzled and wondered, and sometimes were afraid — but they knew that all this great and mysterious world had not come from *nothing*. It had come from God, and he was somehow with them in it.

The wondering did not stop with looking at the moon, the stars, the sun, and the rest of the great world. There was something even more wonderful that God had made. Read in Psalm 8, beginning with verse 3, and see if you can discover God's most wonderful creation. When you have found an answer, read on and see how the writer describes man, this greatest of all God's creation. The Hebrews knew that they too were part of all this. They had not come from nothing, for they were God's own people. Therefore, they sang of the greatness of God who made man in his own likeness.

These words in the psalms are very, very old. You who

hear them now may be very, very young. But the God to whom the Hebrews sang is the God who made you, and all those you love, and the whole wonderful world in which you live. " Nothing comes from *nothing!* "

The Bible is full of songs and words that praise God, that tell of the trust that people have in him, and that call on him for his continuing care and love. People who know that they have come from God know also that God will never stop caring for them or loving them. People who know that they did not come from *nothing* know that the God who made us still rules the world in which he has placed us to live. Even people who do not understand how this can be so know that it is true. Why not sing your own praise to God if you know a favorite hymn? Or you could say your praises as you pray this prayer.

A PRAYER / *Thank you, God, for this wonderful world. Help us to trust in your loving care even when we are puzzled over some of the things that happen to us. Help us to remember that because we are your people, you will never leave us alone. Amen.*

How Old Are You?

HOW OLD ARE YOU? FIVE YEARS OLD — OR TEN — OR EVEN older? Can you remember when you were much younger than you are right now? What did you do? How did you act? How are you different now?

Growing older year by year is lots of fun when you think about all the changing that goes on so that you can do new things. You can skate instead of creep. You can eat hamburgers instead of baby food. You can talk instead of cry.

Growing older is more than fun, however. It means learning to be responsible for acting in more understanding and thoughtful ways toward other people. It means having to

admit to your own mistakes, and being challenged to try to do better. Growing older means having freedom to do more of what you want and less of what someone tells you to do. That means making choices and decisions.

Did you ever stop to think that growing is part of God's plan for every one of the creatures he creates and for every one of his people? If you have a pet dog or cat or hamster or goldfish, think about how it grows and changes. Puppies and kittens with their eyes tightly closed forever could not grow to be dogs and cats that can take care of themselves. They must open their eyes, grow strong, and learn to protect themselves from other animals. Hamsters have baby hamsters that someday grow up and have their own babies. Goldfish, when they are born, are tiny little fish that seldom look as though they could grow to be beautiful golden or blue or black creatures. We wonder about all this as we watch our pets grow and change.

It is even more wonderful to watch boys and girls grow up. If you have a little brother or sister who is just learning to walk, watch him and see what a *big job* walking is! You put one foot up in front . . . and what do you do with the other one? Try walking and thinking about every single step before you take it. That's a lot different from the way you take off running and jumping without thinking about your feet at all, isn't it?

Sometimes when people are acting as though they were younger than they really are, they are told to " act their age." When you try to get attention as you did when you were a baby, or when you refuse to share your toys or pay attention to anyone but yourself, your parents may tell you to " act your age." God wants you to " act your age " too. He wants you to remember how it feels to be shut out or made fun of, so that you will not treat others that way. He wants you to learn to give up your own way sometimes for the good of others. He wants you to learn that acting dishonestly and saying untrue things about other people leads to trouble. He wants you to look around and find ways of being kind and thoughtful. He wants you to enjoy his way of love toward others. He wants you to " act your age."

A PRAYER / *Dear God, sometimes it is hard to " act our age." Help us to learn not to want our own way all the time. Help us to learn how other people feel when we treat them unkindly. Help us to follow the way of love that Jesus taught to his followers. Thank you for your love and forgiveness when we make mistakes or when we do what we know is not " acting our age." Amen.*

" I Could Have Made It Better "

BERT PUSHED HIS NOSE AGAINST THE WINDOW AND BLEW his breath on the glass. He wrote his name in the foggy space where his hot breath had touched the cold glass. Then he pushed his nose against the window again and looked out at the rain. It was running off the roof in a stream, spilling out over the spouts that were supposed to be like little roads for the rain to run down. It was flowing down the street, making it look more like a river than a roadway. Worst of all, the rain was pouring into the river in the center of town so fast that the water would soon be higher than the riverbanks. If the rain did not stop soon, there would surely be a flood!

Bert wondered when his father would get home. He was working on the emergency crew that piled sandbags on the banks every time the river rose high enough to flood the town. The men had been working hard since noontime, trying to pack the bags in rows along the banks to make them higher. If only it would stop raining.

Just then Bert heard the slosh-slosh of rubbers on the porch steps. He ran to the door as his father stepped inside, shaking the water from his rain hat and unbuttoning his heavy coat. He sprinkled Bert with raindrops from his hat.

"Daddy!" shouted Bert. "You're making me all wet."

" Everyone else I know is all wet," laughed Daddy. " You might as well have a few drops too! Where's Mother? "

Mother came in from the kitchen just in time to get a few sprinkles. " Come out and have some coffee," she said. " I've been keeping it hot for you."

Bert drank some milk while Mother and Daddy had coffee. " Did you get the weather news? " asked Father. " Any chance of the rain stopping before midnight? "

Mother shook her head. " It's raining for miles around us," she said. " There is very little hope that it will stop before morning. How are the riverbanks? Will the people down on Water Street have to move out of their homes again? "

Daddy sighed. " If it doesn't stop, they will have to move. A few families have gone already."

" I'm glad we live on this hill," said Bert. " But I want to play baseball. Who can play anything in this kind of weather? If I'd made the world, I'd have made it better than this. . . . I'd have made it so that everyone got enough rain and not too much. I could have made it better, that's what I could have done! "

Daddy rumpled Bert's hair. " Is that so? " he said. " You make it sound like such a simple matter, just enough rain and not a drop too much. Do you know that right now our well has enough water in it for the first time since last spring? The farmers on the edge of town are so happy they are almost ready to go out and dance in the mud, for it's the first time their fields have had a good soaking for months. And down at the coffee shop they are serving everyone a glass of water just to celebrate having enough water to drink! "

" Maybe this will prove to the voters in town that we need money for the dam the state wants to build up the river," said Mother. " I must go down to the church now and see that there is plenty of coffee and food for any of the people who have to move out of their houses. I'm so thankful that we keep emergency supplies on hand for times like this."

When Bert went to bed that night, he could hear the rain

still hitting the roof outside his window. He was still puzzled about why there was too much rain for some people when there was just the right amount for others. Maybe he couldn't have done it better after all, he thought. Maybe he had forgotten that God had given people minds and muscles and money to use in helping others in times of emergency. Maybe there was more to God's plan for the world than Bert had thought!

A PRAYER / *Dear God, we do not always understand that when there is a flood or a bad storm it can be part of your plan for a good world. Help us to think of ways to prevent troubles when we can, and to care for those in need when we cannot do anything about the cause. Amen.*

I Am Wonderfully Made!

RANDY CAME RUNNING INTO THE HOUSE HOLDING HIS NEW saw in one hand while his other hand dripped blood all over the floor and all over Randy! His big brother Max pushed him into the kitchen and told him to put his hand under the water faucet while he washed off the dirt and the blood. Before Randy had time to cry or even worry about what had happened, Max had covered the cut place with a clean bandage. " There you go," said Max. " Did you think your hand was a piece of wood or something? "

Randy looked at the saw. Then he looked at the bandaged hand. " I was just sawing and sawing, and then it slipped and jumped off the wood and started sawing on me! " he said. " Did I cut my hand very much? "

" Not too much," said Max. " Sit down and hold your hand this way while I get some medicine for it." He propped Randy's hand up on the table so that it was up in the air instead of hanging down at his side.

" Why must I hold it this way? " asked Randy, carefully

keeping his hand upright. "What's the medicine for?"

Max brought a bottle of antiseptic, took off the bandage, and carefully patted the cut with cotton dipped in the medicine. "You hold your hand up so that the blood will not be pushing down toward the cut place as hard as it would if you held your hand down. There are hundreds and hundreds of little tubelike vessels all over your body. These are full of blood that travels back and forth from your heart, which beats and pushes it along the vessels. It's a wonderful system, like a network of roads. But when you cut some of them, as you did with your saw, the blood flows out. That means that germs can get in through the cut, and you are losing blood that should be traveling to your heart instead of dripping on the kitchen floor!"

"You mean if I could see inside myself, I could see blood running around all through the tubes," said Randy. "I saw a picture about that in school. But what does this stuff on the cotton do?"

"This kills the germs that are around the cut edges and keeps too many of them from trying to catch a free ride through your blood vessels. They can cause all kinds of trouble, you know. Most of the time, though, the germs are taken care of by the part of your blood that is made to fight them." All the time Max was talking, he was cleaning and bandaging Randy's cut again. "Your body also has a kind of sealer-upper that forms on cut places to patch up the wound until it can start to grow new skin and the blood vessel heals and can carry blood again. I'm telling you, there's nothing like the way a body is put together. It's wonderfully made."

That night when Randy went to bed he looked at his bandaged hand and thought about what Max had told him. "I'm wonderfully made, Mother," he said. Then he told all about the blood vessels and the way the blood works to prevent germs from causing trouble.

Mother brought the Bible from his bookshelf and opened

it to Psalm 139:13-14. "'For thou didst form my inward parts. . . . Wonderful are thy works!'" she read. "Your body is one of the most wonderful of all God's works, Randy. He expects you to take good care of it, and to use it in ways that show that you know it is wonderful."

(Here is the prayer that Randy and his mother prayed that night. You might like to change some of the words and use it as your own.)

A PRAYER / *Thank you, God, that Randy's cut hand is getting better. Thank you for our wonderful bodies that work hard to keep us well and strong. Thank you for doctors and nurses, for medicine and water and everything that helps our bodies do their work when we get hurt. Help us to take good care of our bodies and use them to serve you. Amen.*

God Saw that the World Was Good

HOW DO YOU FEEL WHEN YOU HAVE MADE SOMETHING that took a great deal of time and thought and hard work? Do you look at your finished product, admire it, and want to show someone else how good it is?

In the book called Genesis in the Bible there are two stories about God's creating the world and all the people in it. If you read verse 31 at the end of chapter 1, you will see how the writer describes God's feelings about his work. " And God saw everything that he had made, and . . . it was very good."

Perhaps when you listen to news broadcasts or watch the news on television, you wonder about all the trouble and sad things in the world. Your father may say that things are in a " mess." Mother may think it is a sad world because there are so many hungry people in it. Your friends may say it is not such a good world when rivers flood in the spring and people are forced to leave their homes.

One reason why we believe that the world is good is that we know that God loves his people whom he makes to live in it. If you love someone, you do not give him a " bad " gift or make him live in " bad " places. Think about some of the things God has given us to show his love for us. Can you name something that shows his goodness and caring for us?

Maybe you live where you can see mountains, or the ocean, or a beautiful lake. Maybe the sky is especially blue, or the trees tall and brightly colored in the fall. There may be fish in your lake, good crops in your fields, a horse you can ride, or a puppy you can chase. There is wind for flying kites, playgrounds for playing ball, libraries filled with good books, museums with pictures and interesting exhibits, and food stores full of good things to eat. There are churches where people come together to worship God and to enjoy

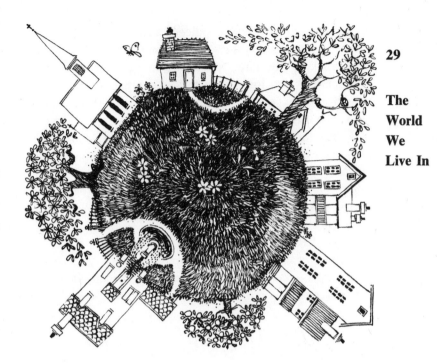

each other's company. There are schools where children learn to use their heads and their hands. There are settlement houses and play groups.

Another way God shows his people that the world is good is by providing many ways for us to be cared for. Some of these ways are right inside ourselves. We learn to talk and ask questions, to speak kindly to others, to ask for directions, and to give advice. Children are born into families who care for them until they can take care of themselves. Sometimes when the families cannot do all the job alone, other people help the children. Fathers have jobs so that they can work and earn money to take care of their families. Sometimes fathers need extra help so that their children can have a place to live and food to eat. There are doctors and hospitals to care for us when we are ill. There are policemen and traffic officers and crossing guards to protect people from others who do not understand that we must all keep the laws. There are many, many ways that God has planned for people to live together in families, in neighborhoods, and in larger communities where we can help each other and be helped in return.

Think about some ways in which you are a part of this plan of caring for others. Are there younger children or older persons who need extra help? Is there someone who cannot talk or walk or see as well as you can? Are you doing your part in God's plan of caring for others?

A PRAYER/ *Thank you, God, for all the people who help to take care of us. Help us to take time to find ways to do our part to care for others. Thank you for making a good world. Amen.*

The Day with No End

MARK WOKE UP SO EARLY THAT NO ONE ELSE IN THE whole house heard him tiptoe to the window and look out to see what kind of day it was. He saw the sun shining on the red bricks of the building across the alley. He saw the blue sky without one single cloud in it. He saw a day that would be perfect for riding his bike, eating a picnic on the grassy field, and playing ball. He saw a day that was just exactly what a holiday should be.

Mark waited patiently for his family to wake up. After everyone had had some breakfast, Mark decided to pack up his chemistry set and put it away for the summer. It was fun to put all the little bottles into a box, to wrap his microscope and put it in a drawer for safekeeping, and to arrange his other materials on the shelf where he could find them when he came back from his summer vacation.

Then Mark decided to ride his bike and see how many of

his friends were going to be in the parade that afternoon. Every child in the neighborhood could decorate his bike or wagon or tricycle and ride around the big circle of road when the little band began to play. Mark joined some of his friends who were already at work cutting paper streamers and taping them to their bike wheels and handlebars. He

decided to use blue crepe paper with some green strips that would fly out in the wind as he rode.

Before Mark knew it, Mother was calling him for lunch. His favorite roast beef sandwich and chocolate milk — and a chocolate brownie for dessert! What a day this was!

Next came the parade, with everybody laughing and clapping and taking pictures of the bikes and wagons and anything that would go on wheels. It was fun to be one of the older children who did not have to ride slowly in a line so that no one would get bumped. It was fun not to be treated like a " little kid."

Then there was a program of singing and games in the big field beside the road. Friends who had not seen each other for several weeks visited and exchanged stories. Little children tumbled over their fathers and older brothers. Mothers put their babies on rugs or blankets in the sunshine. Everyone did just as he pleased. It was great fun!

Best of all was the community picnic where everyone put his dish of food on a long table set up at the edge of the field. Mark took his plate and got in line, sniffing the good smells from up ahead. Soon he had a plate full of good things to eat — even more chocolate brownies!

The boys started a baseball game, and Mark hit a home run his first time up at bat. Everyone was calling him " heavy hitter " and he felt almost like the star of the game.

And then it was time to go home and get ready for bed! " I wish this day could go on forever," said Mark. " I wish it had no end! "

His mother brought him some clean pajamas and sent him off to take a shower. When Mark was ready to climb into bed, Mother said, " Listen while I read what the Bible has to say about a day that would never end. ' For everything there is a season, and a time for every matter under heaven. . . . He has made everything beautiful in its time.' "

Mark snuggled under the covers. " I guess I'd get tired riding a bike or playing ball forever. And I'd get sick if

I kept on eating the way I did at the picnic. Anyway, it feels good to be in this bed, because I'm tired, Mother."

" There's a time to play and a time to sleep," said Mother as she tucked Mark in and turned out the light. " A time to work and a time to rest. Things are good when they are done in their proper time."

A PRAYER / *Thank you, God, for days when we can work and play, and for nights when we can rest. Thank you for making everything good and beautiful in its time. Amen.*

Old World — Or New?

HOW OLD IS THE WORLD? IF YOU TRY TO COUNT BACKWARD in time to the beginnings of things, the numbers get so big they mean hardly anything at all. It's too many years to count! That's why we say that the world is *very* old.

When we say that something is old, we usually mean that it has been around for a long time, or that it has stayed the same for many years. But the world is not quite like that. There is a story about a man named Rip van Winkle who went to sleep for twenty years. When he awoke, he returned to his hometown and was amazed at all the changes that had taken place during his long sleep.

Let's pretend that another Rip van Winkle, who also had been asleep for many years, came back to look at things in this old world. Would he think it was the same old world that he remembered? If you were his guide, you might take him to one of the big airports in the nearest city — and find that he was frightened by the huge " mechanical birds " flying up and out of sight in the sky. You might take him to one of the big expressways — and find that he was frightened by the strange " creatures on wheels." You might take him into your father's dairy barn — and find that he was puzzled by the " mechanical hands " that milk the cows.

The machines in the fields at harvesttime; the television in your home; the telephone; the astronauts in their space suits walking in the weightless, boundless distances of outer space — all these and many other things would make Rip van Winkle ask, " What's going to happen next? " And you would have to answer, " I don't know! "

Our world is never " the same old world." That's why there is no neat set of rules and explanations for everything. As soon as one mystery is explained or one new invention discovered, more of them lie ahead. Sometimes children have trouble explaining to their parents why they must say and do things that are different from the things their father and mother did when they were young. Parents must work hard to understand the world in which their children are growing up, because it is not " the same old world."

Because of all these new and changing things, God's people can never stop wondering and praising him for his great, ongoing work of creation. We give thanks for a world that is always being made new. More important, we must always remember that it is *God's* world, and therefore can never be kept inside the bounds of man's imagination and understanding. God's world is a universe full of mysteries because God intends that his creation shall be greater than all man's possible dreams.

The mysteries of outer space, of unknown persons living on other planets, cures for diseases, the struggle of learning to live with other people — all these and many other mysteries are God's gifts to his people who trust his power and wisdom. We have more knowledge than we know how to use. We shall never know the answers to all our questions. Like Abraham in the long-ago time, God calls us out into a world full of unknown mysteries to live as his people, no matter what we find there. We are called to live as God's men, who are not afraid because we trust him and believe that he loves our world so much that he sent his only Son to make known that love to everyone.

We must not live in fear and terror of what new discovery or event will come next in this old world. Instead, we are to be as trusting as children who know that their Father loves them and will care for them in the midst of the mystery that he creates.

The people in Old Testament times had their own way

of saying " This is God's world! " Read Psalm 24 and try to remember verse 1 so that you can say it from memory. The words will remind you that the world and everything in it, including you, is in God's good care.

A PRAYER / *Thank you, God, that there is always something new in the world. Help us to use our new learning and new skills to make the world the kind of place you want it to be. Help us to learn to live together in it as your faithful children. Amen.*

I Hate the Dark!

MOTHER HAD CALLED BETSY THREE TIMES TO COME AND get ready for bed. Each time Betsy had just one more thing that she *had* to do before she could come. Now Mother was impatient, and Betsy knew that there could be no more excuses. She would *have* to go to bed!

Betsy didn't mind the going to bed part. In fact, she was quite tired, and had almost gone to sleep in the big chair in the living room after supper. What Betsy didn't like was the darkness all around her. When she was at home, Mother always left the little night light burning just outside the door. But here at Aunt Jane's house, there was no night light. Worst of all, Betsy's bedroom was way down the hall from where Mother and Daddy were going to sleep. Betsy was just plain afraid of the dark!

Betsy slowly climbed the stairs to the room where Mother was waiting. She washed her face and hands, put on her pajamas, and jumped into bed. Then she began to cry.

" Why, Betsy, what's the matter? " asked Mother. " Don't you feel well? Tell me about it." Mother sat down on the bed and felt to see if Betsy had a fever.

Betsy wiped her eyes and blinked back the tears. " I hate the dark! " she said. " I just hate it. I'm scared, Mother.

Please let me sleep with the light on tonight."

Mother thought for a moment. Then she said, " Betsy, are you afraid of the sunshine? "

Betsy looked puzzled. " Oh, Mother, of course not! " she said. " I love the sunshine."

Mother said, " Are you afraid when the wind blows? "

"No," said Betsy. " Well, I sort of am afraid when it blows too hard, but then I just come inside."

" Are you afraid of the rain or the snow? " asked Mother.

" I love to walk in the rain, and I love to play in the snow," answered Betsy. " You always have to tell me not to get soaked, Mother."

" All right," said Mother. " You love the sunshine, the wind, the rain, and the snow. You like to swim in the water and you like to climb on the mountains. Who do we believe made all these things, Betsy? "

" Oh, I know that," said Betsy. " It's God's world. He made the sun and the moon and the stars and everything. The sun shines and makes the day, and then it goes down and it gets dark and that's night. That's what I don't like! "

" But if God made the day and cares for us in it, then God also made the night when he also cares for us," said Mother. " The day is God's and the night is his also. The day is for working and playing. The night is for resting and sleeping. It takes the two of them together to make things right for people."

" I guess I didn't think much about the night being God's, too," said Betsy. " I was too busy hating it. I'll try, Mother. I'll say to myself, ' The night is God's also.' "

" There's a verse in our Bible that says the same thing," said Mother. " It says, ' Thine is the day, thine also is the night.' I'll show you where to find it in the morning and you can read it for yourself. Good night now, Betsy. It's time for prayers."

(You can read the verse in Psalm 74:16. The word " luminaries " could be changed to " moon " and " stars.")

A PRAYER / *We give thanks, O God, for day and night. As you care for us in the daytime, when we can see all about us, we know that you also care for us at night, when it is dark and we cannot see. Thank you that the dark does not hide us from you. Thank you for your love and care that are alike in daytime and at nighttime, for " dark and light are both alike to thee." Amen.*

The Magic of Tiny Things

WHAT DO YOU THINK OF WHEN SOMEONE TALKS ABOUT THE wonderful world that God has made? Giant trees, brilliant sunsets, mighty rivers, or high mountain peaks? Or do you think of snowflakes that are all of different designs, flowers with their many parts, or hummingbirds whose wings move so fast you can hardly see them?

There are some verses in Proverbs 6:6-8 that will make you stop and think about one tiny bit of magic in God's world. If you do not have time right now to read them, here is what they tell you to do: Go and see how the tiny ants work hard all summer in order to gather food enough to last

all winter. They have no one ruling over them or ordering them about. Think about their ways, and try to learn something from the ants!

Who would think that ants are good teachers? Who goes around looking at ants in order to become wise? Ants are the things that get into our food at picnics, or that scurry about when we dig up their hills. They are mostly something we want to get rid of as fast as we can.

Maybe the writer of Proverbs knew something about ants that you don't know. Do you know that ants always live together in colonies, so they have to get along together? It can't be " every ant for himself "! Do you know that there may be as many as thirty-five or forty queens in one colony? Queens in beehives are very jealous of each other, and each one wants to be *the* ruler. Ant queens are not like that. They seem to act as though every queen should share the job of laying eggs and making a home. So they live together peaceably, and the ant colonies grow and grow. Do you think that the writer of Proverbs saw any wise teachings for men and women in the ways of the ant?

The next time you see ants running about on the sidewalk or in the dirt, stop to watch them. At first they look as though they are going every which way, getting nowhere at all. If you watch carefully, however, you will see that they may be carrying something, or pulling and pushing another tiny insect. They are hard at work laying in a supply of food for the colony. Do you know that ants keep " herds " of tiny insects that are often called " ant cows " (their real name is *aphids*) because the ants " milk " them by stroking their backs so that they will give off a sweet fluid that the ants drink as if it were milk. All the ants have some kind of work to do, and they keep very busy doing it. Do you think the writer of Proverbs knew this?

You might like to look around you and see if there are other creatures that can teach us some lessons. Watch a robin building a nest. Try to find where a squirrel is storing nuts for the winter. See how the mother cat cares for her kittens. Try writing your own " proverb " like the one in Proverbs 6:6-8. If this writer had lived today, he might have said:

> Go and watch the ant, you lazy bones!
> Look at the way she gets along with other
> ants, and see if you can't learn a lesson
> from that.
> Notice how she gathers food, and how every
> ant works at some job without a boss
> watching and checking all the time.
> If ants can do that, why can't people?

A PRAYER / *Your world is full of wonderful things, dear God. Thank you for your wise plan for all living things. Help us to learn from even the tiny insects that each of us has work to do, and that doing it well is part of your plan for us. Help us to understand that living together happily takes work and thoughtfulness and sharing on everybody's part. Thank you for your love, O God. Amen.*

Growing Up

WHAT DO YOU THINK IS THE HARDEST PART OF GROWING up? Do you ever wish you were the youngest in your family, or that you were a small child again so that you would get more attention? Do you ever wish that you were older so that you could be your own boss? Do you ever wish that you looked like someone else? or that you lived in some other family?

Sometimes we cause our own " growing up " problems. When you were very young, your mother probably said to

you, " Don't touch the stove. It is hot. It will burn you."
Do you remember ever thinking that you would like to touch
the stove, just to be sure that it was hot, as your mother said?
or thinking that you would touch the stove anyway, just because you wanted to do that? Or maybe you decided to
touch the stove just because your mother told you not to!
Whatever the reason, do you remember how it felt when
you burned your finger? Your mother may have said, " I told
you not to touch the stove! I hope you have learned a lesson."

Your mother and father know that there are many things
that you will want to do that will cause results you will be
sorry for afterward. When you are " growing up " it is hard
to listen when they tell you about such things. It seems like
more fun to do what you want to do, and to " try it and
see " if the results are what your parents warned you about.

Jesus helps people to " grow up " if they will listen to his
words and learn from his life. He tried to show people that
living together in a way that shows we love and respect each
other brings better results than when we show hatred and
selfishness toward them. He also helps us to understand that
when we do follow his way, we will not always be thanked
for it. Sometimes we may wonder whether we have done the
right thing. Sometimes the people we treat kindly and with
respect do not seem to like what we do. Jesus says that it is
part of " growing up " to keep on showing kindness and love
even when it is not returned to us. Not receiving love in return does not excuse anyone from trying to show love to
others. Jesus also reminds us that there is someone who loves
us so much that he returns to us far more love than we can
ever give to him. You know who that is, don't you? It is God.

Jesus also helps people in " growing up " by making clear
that God loves each of his people just the way they are.
Others may be more beautiful, get better grades in school,
have more friends, or get a bigger allowance. That doesn't
matter to God. He intends you to be your own self, and to

make the best use of all that he has given to you. He has a particular plan for your life, and no one else can take your special place. God does not wish that you were someone else. He made you to be YOU!

You might like to pray this prayer when you feel that " growing up " is not so great after all!

A PRAYER / *Dear God, when I am tired trying to convince my parents to let me do what I want to do, help me to remember that they love me and are doing what they think is best for me. When I wish I were someone else, help me to remember that you love me as I am. When I make mistakes and do things I wish I had not done, help me to remember that you are ready to forgive me and help me to " grow up " in trust and obedience to your way of love. Amen.*

Whose Dollar Is It?

BECKY AND BENNY WERE TWINS. ON THEIR BIRTHDAY THE packages that their mother and father gave them were always marked " Becky " and another one " Benny." That was because Daddy said that separate people ought to have separate presents! Mother said that it stopped any argument over who would open the packages!

On this birthday, an envelope came in the mail and was addressed to " Becky and Benny." Becky opened it, because Benny didn't care much about opening envelopes. He couldn't read the writing on the cards and letters that were always inside. Opening envelopes wasn't much fun for Benny.

But this envelope was different. Inside, Becky found a funny card shaped like the cashier's window at the bank where Daddy kept the family money between paydays. She pulled the little tab that said " Pull," and out came a crisp, new one-dollar bill. It was a birthday present from the man who had stayed in their house while he was doing some work in Daddy's office.

"Look, Benny," called Becky, waving the dollar bill in the air. "We have a dollar for our birthday."

"Let's spend it," said Benny. "I want to buy a shovel to dig fishing worms."

"I don't want to spend my money yet," said Becky. "I have to think about what I want."

"It's mine as much as yours," yelled Benny. "Give me my birthday money."

"I won't! It's mine too, and I'll keep it as long as I want to," shouted Becky.

Just then their big brother Bob came into the room where the twins were shouting at each other. "Stop it, you two!" he said firmly. "What is this fuss all about? Whose dollar is that?"

"It's mine!" said Benny.

"It's mine too," said Becky. "It's our birthday dollar."

"Why don't you put it in my box here?" said Bob. "I'm collecting money for the new hospital. If we don't collect plenty today, we may not be able to start the building."

The twins looked at each other. Then they looked at Bob. Give away their whole dollar? They couldn't do that!

Bob grinned at the twins. "Remember the verse that you two learned at church school yesterday? You bragged all the way home about being the first ones to be able to say it from memory."

"'The earth is the Lord's and the fulness thereof, the world and those who dwell therein,'" said the twins together.

"What's that got to do with our dollar?" asked Benny.

"I know," said Becky. "It's like Miss Patton said in church school. The things in the world are ours to use, but we don't really own them because the world and everything in it belongs to God. We can *use* this dollar, but we don't really *own* it."

"Maybe we could give a little bit of it to the hospital,"

said Benny. " I had to go way off to West Newton when I had my tonsils out."

" That's a good idea! " said Becky. " I'll give ten cents."

" I will too," said Benny. " How much does that leave? "

" Thanks, twins," said Bob. " Here's your change. Forty cents for each of you. I guess you *learned* that verse — you didn't just memorize some words! "

(The verse the twins learned is Psalm 24:1. You can read it in your own Bible. Think about the difference between *owning* something and being given something to *use as you please.*)

A PRAYER / *Dear God, thank you for all your good gifts to us. Help us to use them wisely, and to remember that you have given us what really belongs to you. Amen.*

God's Eyes

" HOW MANY EYES DOES GOD HAVE, DADDY? " ASKED PETER.

Daddy looked up from his newspaper. " How many *eyes?* What do you mean, Peter?"

" I just want to know how many eyes God has," insisted Peter. " Does he have two? Or does God have a lot of eyes? "

Daddy put down the paper. " No one has ever seen God, Peter, so if I said that God definitely has two eyes, I would be telling you something that no one knows. When people picture God, they usually describe him as we describe human beings. That's not with a lot of eyes instead of two eyes! Why do you ask about God's eyes? "

"Well," said Peter stretching out on the floor, "Larry said that there was a place in the Bible that said God had a whole lot of eyes. It said that God had so many eyes that they were in every place. Is that true, Daddy? Does God have that many eyes?"

Peter's father went to the bookshelf and took down the Bible. "I think I know what Larry is talking about," he said. "Here it is, in Proverbs 15:3. Read what it says."

Peter read: "'The eyes of the Lord are in every place, keeping watch on the evil and the good.'"

"I think that the 'keeping watch' part is more important than how many eyes God has," said Daddy. "You see, the long-ago writers often wrote as though they were painting pictures. We sometimes say they were painting word pictures, and we do the same thing ourselves. Let's see, what do I mean when I say that I am able to tell when it is a good time to start building houses in a part of town where no one lives yet because I 'keep my ear to the ground'? Have you ever seen me crawling around with my ear really down on the ground?"

Peter laughed and laughed. "Try it, Daddy! Try crawling around with your ear on the ground."

Daddy tried, and rolled right over on the floor beside Peter! They both laughed so hard they were out of breath when Daddy finally got back up into his chair.

"About God's eyes," said Daddy when he was at last able to talk. "The Hebrews knew that they could not hide any of their acts from God. They could not even hide the feelings that were deep down inside. God saw what was good, and he saw what was evil. When they put this into words, and when they said that God 'saw' something, they thought of 'eyes'! When they said that God's eyes are in every place, they were really saying that nothing can be

hidden from God."

" I'd rather God couldn't see the evil part," said Peter. " I'd like him to see the good."

" It's not very pleasant to go around trying to hide something evil even from another person," said Daddy. " God wants his people to love him and trust him. He does not want them to try to hide anything from him. Instead, he wants us to know that he sees and understands our mistakes and the wrongs that we do, and that he still loves us and wants to help us to follow his way of love instead. You can't trust God's love and ask his forgiveness, and at the same time think that you are hiding from him the reasons why you need to be forgiven."

" I guess you're right," said Peter. " Maybe if we didn't think God knew all about us, we might be afraid that sometimes he wouldn't know where we were. Then he couldn't help us. I'm glad his eyes are all over the place."

" '. . . keeping watch,' " said Daddy. " Don't forget that part. God watches over us and cares for us all the time wherever we are. Don't ever forget that, Peter."

A PRAYER / *Thank you, God, that we can never go out of your sight. Thank you for knowing when we do evil and for forgiving us. Thank you for knowing when we are acting in love toward others. Help us not to try to hide our mistakes from you, but always to be honest and to ask for your forgiveness. Thank you that we can always trust in your loving care no matter where we go. Amen.*

Darkness and Light

PERHAPS IT IS DAYLIGHT WHEN YOU ARE READING THIS book. Or did you have to turn on a light in order to see? Have you ever been sitting inside a house during a thunderstorm at night, and suddenly have all the lights go out? How did you feel? Have you ever turned on a light and have the bulb burn out and the room go dark? When was the last time you wanted light to see by, but were not able to have it?

Light is one of the things that we have all about us and seldom give any thought to. In the morning we wake up and it is daylight. Even in the wintertime, the sky is getting lighter even though it seems dark inside the house. We walk into a room at night, snap on an electric switch, and the room is full of light. We go to the beach in the summer, and the light from the sun is so bright that we put on sunglasses. We pull down the blinds or draw the curtains to keep light out of our bedroom if we want to sleep late in the morning.

Think of some things you could not do if there were no light. How would you play games after dark if you could not turn on lights in your house? How could your parents drive along dark roads at night without headlights on the car? How could people work at night without lights? How could doctors and nurses perform operations without bright lights that help them to see well?

Light is very important in our lives. The word " light " is often used in the Bible. Jesus once told his followers that they were " the light of the world," and like the lights of a city perched high up on a hill. A traveler coming from far off would certainly be able to see the lights, for they could not be hidden. You can read these verses in Matthew 5:14-16.

How can *people* be like *lights?* Think first about all the things that light makes it possible for you to do. Without

light you would be prevented from doing much that makes your life useful and happy. Light enables you to see where you are going and what you are doing. Jesus wanted people to understand that his teachings were meant to help them see where to go and what to do. Jesus wanted to make clear to people God's expectation for them. He wanted people to see how to move toward God and do his will. He wanted to turn the light of understanding on in the minds and hearts of people. He said that he was the light of the world that would take away the darkness of not knowing God and his ways. (John 8:12.)

The light that Jesus speaks of includes all those things which help us know and understand God's plan for his people. Each one of us at some time will be able to make clear something of that plan. When we show love and kindness to others, that is making clear to them a little of God's way of love. When we forgive those who do us wrong, we are shedding a little light on God's way of forgiveness. When we trust God and obey him, we are letting the light of our belief in him shine so that others can understand better that God's love is for them.

You have a choice to make about whether or not you will bring light or darkness about God's love. You can either make God's way clear by your own acts of faithful obedience, or you can hide his way by acting selfishly and without love. You can make known your belief in God through living in trust, or you can pretend that God does not exist and that you alone run your life. You are important, because you can be a " light." Therefore, do not let your light be hidden.

A PRAYER / *Dear God, help us to remember that we are like lights that can help to give direction to people who see the way we act and hear the way we speak. Give us light, that we may know what is good and right for us to do. Thank you for Jesus, who is the Light that makes our life worth living. Amen.*

I Want to Go Home!

MARY LOU SAT ON THE TOP STEP OF THE PORCH AT UNCLE Bill's house and looked down the long street. Then she looked up the long street.

If I were at home, Jeannie or somebody would be coming down the street to play with me, thought Mary Lou. There's no one to play with here.

Mary Lou got up from the step and went inside to the kitchen. Aunt Maud was baking cookies. My mother would have asked me to help her, thought Mary Lou. I wish I were at home with my mother.

" Have a fresh cookie, Mary Lou," said Aunt Maud. " They're chocolate chip."

" That's my favorite kind," said Mary Lou as she bit into a cookie. " But these don't have any oatmeal in them! I like oatmeal chocolate chip cookies best."

Mary Lou went outside again to look for the doll that she had left on the porch step. Chipper the puppy had pulled the doll across the porch and was chewing on one of her new white shoes. " Let go, Chipper. Get away. I don't like you," said Mary Lou. " My dog, Puff, doesn't chew things up. I wish I were back home."

All that day Mary Lou went around looking gloomy. I didn't want to come to stay with Uncle Bill anyway, she thought. I wouldn't have been in the way at home, even if

Mother does have to spend all her time taking care of our new little baby. I would help Mother. I want to go home!

That night Aunt Maud came to tuck Mary Lou into bed. " We're glad you are staying with us for a while," said Aunt Maud. " I think we can go to the zoo tomorrow, if you'd like."

Mary Lou pulled up the covers. She tried not to look at Aunt Maud. And then she started to cry. " I don't want to go to the zoo," she sobbed. " I want to go home."

Aunt Maud pushed back Mary Lou's hair and patted her head. " It's hard to be in a strange house in a strange town without your own friends, dear," she said. " But there are good things here that you should try to enjoy. Uncle Bill and I love you very much, Mary Lou, and we want to make you happy. And even though you are in a different house in another town from your mother and father, you know that they are loving you and thinking about you all the time. Their love is with you here, just as it is at home."

Mary Lou wiped her eyes. " I guess I didn't think about it like that," she said. " I just thought about not being able to see them and be with them. I kept wanting to go home. But I'd like to go to the zoo, Aunt Maud. Can we see the baby bear cubs?"

" Yes, indeed we can," said Aunt Maud. " And now it's time for you to get to sleep so you'll have lots of energy for walking around our big zoo. It's one of the biggest zoos anywhere! "

The next morning at breakfast, Uncle Bill opened the Bible to read what he called " God's word for us today." While he was looking for the place, he said, " I am going to read what some people said once long ago when they were living far away from home in a strange land where everything was different from what they were used to. They thought that because they were not able to worship in their own Temple in Jerusalem, God was no longer with them. They wanted more than anything else to get back home and to be where they thought God was. Here is what they said: ' By the waters of Babylon, there we sat down and wept, when we remembered Zion. . . . How shall we sing the Lord's song in a foreign land? ' "

" Did they get back home? " asked Mary Lou, eager to know more about them.

Uncle Bill nodded. " Yes, they did. But they learned that God was with them even in the faraway foreign land. His love and care are never in one certain place, but are always with his people wherever they go."

" Like my mother's and daddy's love is with me," said Mary Lou.

Aunt Maud smiled. " That's the greatest thing about love," she said. " It can be anywhere and everywhere with us, all the time."

Mary Lou slid off her chair. " I'm finished," she said. " Let's go to the zoo."

(The verses that Uncle Bill read from the Bible are in Psalm 137:1, 4.)

A PRAYER / *Thank you, God, for your love that goes with us always. Help us to love each other, and to show our love in thoughtful and kind ways. Thank you that we can never go so far away from those who love us that their love is gone from us. Thank you most of all for Jesus, who shows us how great your love for us is. Amen.*

Is God Listening?

BETH RAN UP THE BACK STAIRS, STOOD VERY STILL IN THE hallway, and called in a loud voice, " Hello, God! " She listened and listened, but all that she could hear was the rain blowing against the windows. Beth shook her head sadly and walked slowly down the stairs.

" Mother! " she called.

" H'mmmm? " said Mother.

" Where are you? " asked Beth.

" I'm in here, writing a thank-you note to Aunt Grace for the candy she sent us at Christmas. Did you want something, Beth? " answered Mother.

" I was just calling on God, Mother . . . only he can't hear me," said Beth. " I even went upstairs where it's quiet, but I guess the rain must be making too much noise! "

Mother looked up from her letter. " What do you mean you were calling on God, Beth? "

" Well, you and Daddy are always saying that people can call on God when they need something — and I needed something in a hurry, so I called on him. When I call you, Mother, you always say, ' H'mmmm ' or something. And Daddy always says, ' Yes? ' If God hears people, why doesn't he say something when I call on him, Mother? " asked Beth.

Mother thought for a moment. " God's way of answering when we call is different from Daddy's or mine," she said. " Different people have different ways of answering."

" But you and Daddy always say *something*, Mother," Beth insisted. " Even if you only ask me, ' What? ' I know you've heard me. Or if you just look up, I can *see* that you heard me! "

" That's what makes your question so hard to answer," said Mother. " When we call on God, we cannot see him as you see Daddy and me. We cannot hear him answer, either, as you hear us. But we *know* that he hears and answers our prayers, Beth."

" How do we know he really hears? " asked Beth. " I'd like to hear God say, ' H'mmmmm ' just once when I called on him! "

" You're not the only person who has felt that way," said Mother with a smile. " I guess I've felt something like that myself a few times, but I know God hears, because he an-

swers my prayers."

" You mean God's way of showing us he hears is by answering our prayers? " asked Beth.

" That's one very important way," said Mother. " Another way is found in our Bible. It tells us over and over again how God wants his people to love him and trust him, and to come to him for help as well as to give him thanks and praise. If God did not intend to listen to his people, do you think he would tell them to call upon him? Especially when we know how faithful he has been about always keeping his promises? "

" You mean the Bible is sort of one way that God has of saying, ' H'mmmm? ' to us? " laughed Beth.

" Right you are," said Mother. " My ' H'mmmm ' doesn't really say anything that you could call an answer, does it? "

" No," said Beth. " But I know you always do listen, and you love me, and you try to do whatever you can to *really* give me an answer — like when I want something, and all that."

" Then you expect Daddy and me to listen and answer because you know we have always done this, and you know we want to do what is best for you because we love you," said Mother. " That's why it is so important for all of us to know God, to understand the great love he has for us, and to trust him to listen and answer us because he loves us. Jesus came to tell us and show us that so that we need never doubt God's love again. And if we do not doubt his love, then we do not have to doubt that he hears us when we call on him."

" You make it sound so real! " said Beth. " You really mean it, don't you, Mother? "

" Yes, I do mean it, dear," said Mother. " I know I can't explain it all so that you will understand exactly *how* God listens and answers our prayers. He asks us to trust him, and to have faith in him. I guess that's what I'm asking you to do . . . and to try God out. Then you will find out for yourself, in a way that no one else can explain in words."

That night when Beth was ready for bed, Daddy came in to kiss her good night. " Mother told me about your talk today," he said. " Here are some verses that tell us what Jesus taught his disciples about how much more God wants to give his children good gifts in answer to their prayers than even parents do." Then Daddy read to her the verses you can read in your Bible in Matthew 7:7-12. If you talk

about these with your parents, they can help you understand more of what Jesus was telling us about God.

A PRAYER / *Thank you, God, for wanting us to come to*
you with our prayers. Help us to understand your ways of
listening to us and answering us. Help us to know you so
that we can trust you and love you more and more. Amen.

The Earth Is the Lord's

JOHN'S KNIFE WAS SHINY AND SHARP. IT HAD A BIG, WIDE
blade that would cut right through a thick tree branch . . .
zing! It was a good knife to use when he went camping with
the Boy Scouts or when his family went off in their trailer to
a tent camp. It was a very good knife for cutting things!

" I wonder if my knife would cut through the bark of that
tree behind the house? " asked John one day. " What good is
a knife if you are not sure what it will cut? I'll try it and find
out."

John made one big gash, then another, and he was about
to cut into the tree a third time when Father's voice called,
" John, you are not cutting that tree, are you? "

John looked at his knife, and he looked at the tree. " Yes,
Father, but I was only trying out my knife," he said. " I'm
not cutting it down. I won't cut it any more."

Father came to look at the tree. " Oh, John," he said.
" You must never cut into a tree. We must take care of these
slashes at once. Run to the garage and get the can that is on
the table beside the door. Bring it to me and we will fix the
cuts."

John did as his father asked, and watched carefully while
he smeared the black, sticky paint all over the cut places in
the bark.

" There," said Father. " See how I covered every little

opening in the cuts, John? That's to keep out anything that might allow disease to get inside the tree."

" It's like a big Band-Aid! " said John. " Only it's black instead."

" A tree can heal itself just as your body can," said Father. " You have to give it a chance, though. You have to take care of it. It takes a long time for a tree to grow big and tall like this one, but disease can kill it in a very short time. That's why you should never slash it, or any tree, unless you plan to cut it down and make good use of it."

" It's all right to cut trees for firewood," said John. " And for lumber — and sticks for toasting marshmallows."

" God gave us trees to use in many ways," said Father. " He expects us to use them wisely, however, and not to cut too many in one place or to cut them before they are ready. I'm sure God does not intend for us to waste his trees, either."

" I always thought this was *our* tree," said John. " Could you cut it down if you wanted to? "

" Yes, I could cut it down," said Father. " But since God's world includes this tree, and God expects me to treat his world wisely, he must expect me to have a good reason for cutting down my tree. I do not think he would be pleased if I hacked it down because I was angry about something, or if I cut it down without thinking what I was doing. The Bible says it this way:

> The earth is the Lord's and the fulness
>   thereof,
> the world and those who dwell therein.
>   (Psalm 24:1.)

John looked at his shiny, sharp knife. He looked at the black ring around the tree. " I'll think about that before I cut any more trees," he said. " I'll try to remember whose trees they really are."

A PRAYER / *Dear God, thank you for the wonderful world that you have made. Help us to remember that the earth is yours, and that you expect us to treat it with care. Amen.*

Make My Dog Get Better

PETER AND BING RACED EACH OTHER DOWN THE STREET and into the vacant lot where the gang was playing baseball. Bing was Peter's puppy, and the mascot of the team. Bing never missed a game, and he always barked when Peter got a hit.

Peter's friend Rick hit a long, high ball that went out over the bushes and into the street. Peter chased after it, with Bing at his heels. Just as Peter picked up the ball, a car came down the street just a little faster than it should have been going. The driver was watching Peter, but did not see Bing.

"Yip! Yip! Yip!" went Bing as he rolled over and over in the street. Then he lay very still and didn't make any sound at all.

All the boys gathered around while Peter picked Bing up and started for home. No one knew whether Bing was badly hurt, or whether the car wheel had just bumped him. Rick ran on ahead to tell Peter's mother, and she was waiting at the driveway with the car keys when the others arrived.

" Put Bing on the blanket in the back seat, and we will take him to the vet right away," she said. " You can tell me what happened later."

In a few minutes the doctor was checking him over carefully. " I'm not exactly sure what is wrong yet," he said. " I will keep Bing here tonight and then I will call you in the morning to tell you how badly he is hurt. Don't worry, Peter, I'll take good care of Bing."

As they drove back home, Peter was very quiet. He felt funny in his stomach. What if Bing didn't get well? What if the doctor forgot to watch over him? What if Bing got hungry and no one fed him?

Peter didn't eat much supper that evening. When everyone else had finished, Peter's father said, " Let's sit on the porch for a little while. It's cooler, and I think it's going to rain."

Peter sat down on the top step. " Father," he said, " when Betsy got hurt on the swings at school, you said that you and Mother prayed for her to get well."

" That's right," said Father. " And you did too, I remember."

" Do you think it would be all right with God if I prayed for Bing to get better? " asked Peter.

" I think any real prayer is all right with God, Peter, but I think you should know what you are praying about and be sure you mean what you say," said Father thoughtfully.

" I'd like God to make Bing get better right away," said Peter. " That's what I mean really."

" Let's think about that a minute," said Father. " In the first place, I think you are forgetting that God's plan for the creatures that he has made includes some wonderful healing that has already begun in Bing. His body is working hard and fighting the disease germs and doing many amazing things without anyone else's help. That's God at work making him better right now."

" The doctor is probably giving him shots," said Peter.

" That will help him fight the germs."

" Right you are," said Father. " That's some more of God's plan. Doctors and scientists use their minds to find out reasons for diseases and hurt places, and they work to find some cures or helps."

" When Bing comes home, I'll take good care of him," said Peter. " That's God's plan too, isn't it? Pets need some-

one to take care of them because they can't do it all themselves."

"I think you get what I mean," said Father. "When you ask God to help Bing get better, you might include a 'Thank you' that so much is being done already. Remember, Peter, that God is not someone we are to order around, no matter how much we want something."

"I guess I'll not just say, 'Make my dog better' when I pray about Bing. I'll sort of talk it over with God so I don't forget he's taking care of him right now," said Peter.

A PRAYER / *Dear God, thank you that your plan for the world includes care for our pets. Help us to take good care of them. When they get hurt, help us to remember that they are your creatures too, and that your way of caring for them is already at work. Amen.*

What Is "Always"?

"WE *always* HAVE CHOCOLATE CAKE ON BIRTHDAYS AT our house," said Mitzi.

"We *always* have ice cream on birthdays," said Janet.

"You had yellow cake on Sammie's birthday," said Bill.

"Oh, well, that was because Mother ran out of chocolate and the store was closed. That was only once!" said Mitzi.

"Then you don't *always* have chocolate cake," insisted Bill.

"Once we couldn't have ice cream because the electricity was off when there was a bad storm," said Janet. "But we always have it other times."

"That's not *always*," said Bill. "That's sometimes — or maybe even most times. But that's not the same as *always*."

"Don't be silly," said Janet. "There's nothing that's absolutely *always!*"

" Well, I don't know about that," said Mitzi. " My father is always — I mean lots of times — my father says that something is as sure as night follows day. That's *always!* "

" Sure," said Bill, " and the sun *always* comes up in the morning to make daylight. The moon *always* comes at night."

" Sometimes you can see the moon in the daytime," said Janet. " But it *always* gets large and small every month. The pictures of it are on our calendar. You can even find out in the almanac when it's going to be big and when it will be like a little sliver."

" I know a funny *always,*" said Mitzi. " It *always* stops raining! "

"Spring *always* comes after winter, and then summer and fall," said Bill. " All people don't have cold winters where they live, though."

" It is *always* cold for a long time near the North Pole," said Janet. " My brother was there in the army. He wore fur gloves! "

" People *always* stick onto the earth, even though it's whirling around terribly fast," said Mitzi. " That's gravity."

" Not if you get far enough away you don't," said Bill. " But the scientists are discovering some *always's* in outer space too. I don't know what they are yet."

" The real *always's* are the kind we don't do anything about," said Janet. " Like the sun and the moon, and seasons, and what makes the world go around and us not fall off . . . and the rain stop, and all that."

" That's because God made the world, and he made it so that we could count on it," said Bill. " That's what my father says. He says that we should stop to think sometimes about all the things that are *sure* because God made them, and that men can't go around mixing things up even if they want to."

" There's one *always* my mother is always talking about," said Mitzi. " She's always saying to all of us — I mean lots of times — she's saying, ' I will *always* love you, no matter what happens.' She means it, too. She says if love is real, you should be able to count on it."

" Mr. Biggs said in church on Easter that that's what the celebrating is all about. It's because God's love is *always* with us and *always* wins out over everything, even death," said Bill. " He said we could add a word to one of the Bible verses we learned, and it would be all right. We could say, ' God is love ' — *always!* "

" It seems that God is the only one who can make an *always*," said Janet.

" I'm glad he made the world instead of leaving it to us. Maybe it would be like the chocolate cake — just a some-time always. And that's no *always* at all! " said Bill.

A PRAYER / *Thank you, God, for loving us always. Thank you for making a world that we can depend on. Teach us to praise your name for all your good gifts to us. Amen.*

Don't Blame God

MARK'S FATHER TOLD HIM NOT TO PLAY BALL NEAR THE old building that the workmen were tearing down. The glass in the windows was loose, and pieces kept falling out when a truck or bus went by in the street. Mark liked to throw his ball against the wall. When he knew his father would not see him, he played ball against the wall. A big piece of window glass fell out, hit Mark on the head, and cut his face. That night when Mark went to bed he said, " I'm not going to pray to God to keep me safe. He let me get cut by the window glass. God didn't answer my prayer."

Do you think Mark was right? If God gave Mark a mind that could understand the danger his father had pointed out to him, and if he had a father who warned him, was it God's fault that Mark was hurt? What kind of world would this be if glass that was jiggled loose by the rumble of a heavy truck stopped falling and hung in midair because God decided to act like a magician to keep Mark from getting hurt?

Ruth liked bananas. She ate so many bananas that her family teased her by calling her a monkey. Her mother warned her not to eat too many of them at one time or she might get a stomachache. One day Ruth saw a bowl full of bananas that her mother had just brought from the store. She ate five of them, one right after the other as fast as she could so that no one would catch her eating them. When her mother found her, she was curled up in a big chair crying because — you're right! She had a stomachache. Ruth said, " I don't think God should have made things that make people sick when they eat them! "

Do you agree with Ruth? When God created the world for man's good, do you think God counted on man to use his gifts wisely? Who was to blame for Ruth's stomachache?

In a town that had been built along a riverbank many, many years ago, there were people whose houses were always being flooded when the water rose in the spring. Ev-

ery time the leaders of the town asked the people to vote to raise some money to help build a dam up the river, to keep the water from rising too fast, the people voted no. " We don't want to spend our money on a dam," they said. " We want to spend it on ourselves."

Every year when the waters began to rise, the people who

had voted no about spending money for the dam would gather in someone's house. There they would pray, sometimes for hours at a time, that God would not let the water rise and flood their homes. When the floods came, many of the people would say, " There's no use praying to God for help. Look at our houses. They are full of mud and water. God must not care about his people to send rain and floodwaters like this down on us."

Are the people right to blame God for the floods? Do you think that part of God's answer to their prayers was the idea about building a dam?

Think what a mixed-up world it would be if God kept changing it around to suit everyone's wish at the moment. Today you would want the sun to shine so that you could go on a picnic, and someone else would like it not to shine so that the weather would be cooler. A farmer might want summer to last two months longer so that he could harvest a better crop, and the manager of a ski resort would want winter to come two months earlier so that he could make more money. God's world is not made according to man's wishes. His world is sure and orderly, and he expects man to learn to live in it and use its gifts wisely and for the good of everyone.

Read Psalm 8:3-9. Think about the things that God has made for man's use in this wonderful, orderly world which he created.

A PRAYER / *Thank you, God, that you do not change the world around to suit our wishes. Thank you for giving us minds that help us understand how to use your good gifts. Teach us to make wise decisions and good choices about using all that you have made. Amen.*

God and His People

II

I AM THE LORD YOUR GOD. . . . YOU SHALL have no other gods before me." These familiar words from Exodus 20:2a, 3, pose a real problem for children who are living in a time very far indeed from the days of Moses and the Children of Israel. They are easy words to learn to say from memory, but they are not easy ideas to comprehend. Who is this God who commands us to give our lives into his care, and his alone? How do we know that it is enough to put all our trust in him and in no other gods?

The early Hebrews were asking the same kinds of questions about God. In every age, man has asked, " Who is God? " " What is he like? " " What can he do? " " Does he care about me? " The Bible contains the story of God's mighty acts by which he made himself known to his people, for God does not choose to hide from his people, thus placing the burden of the search upon them. Instead, he reaches out and takes the initiative in revealing himself in all his wisdom, power, and love. Time after time he speaks through his actions and words to say to people in every generation, " I am God! "

It is well to remember that God intends his people to wonder and ask questions about him. He wants us to see what he has done through his dealings with his people, and what he is doing in Christ for man's salvation. God wants us to love him, but he leaves man free to choose whether or not to respond in obedience and trust. In the following readings, questions about God and his dealings with his people long ago and today are raised and examined. These will no doubt lead to other puzzling problems, some of which you will be able to answer. Others will require that you and your children search out some answers together. Still others will remain among those unanswerable questions, the answers to which are not for man to comprehend at this time. In every case, the primary concern should be to allow God's revelation of himself to hold the center of the stage.

Children deserve to understand what a struggle it was for

God's people to trust and obey him, and to be the kind of people he intends them to be. Then they may recognize some similarity to their own efforts to do what is right and loving as they respond to God's love and care for them today.

Who Is the Real Ruler?

HAVE YOU EVER WONDERED WHETHER OR NOT GOD IS strong enough to *do something* about all the troubles in the world today? Have you ever wondered whether a dictator, a king, or a president might become so powerful that nothing could stop him from making wrong decisions or bringing harm to people? There are many stories in the Bible that seem to be there just to answer questions like these.

One of these stories is about a king named Ahab who ruled in Israel a long time ago. Next door to his palace was a beautiful vineyard belonging to a man named Naboth. Like his father and grandfather before him, Naboth had worked hard to make the vineyard produce big, sweet, juicy grapes. While they were getting ripe, he watched from a little tower in the middle of the vineyards to see that no foxes came to destroy his grapes. Often as Naboth stood guard, he would see King Ahab watching him from the palace. Then Naboth would grow sad, for he knew that the king did not love the Lord God as he should. Ahab had married a

wife from another land, where the people did not believe in the one true God. Now Ahab was no longer faithful to God either. Surely it was a troublesome time.

One day the king came to visit Naboth. " I want this vineyard of yours for my own," he said. " I want to make a vegetable garden here near my palace. I will pay you well for it. Choose whether you want me to give you a better vineyard, or its value in money."

Naboth hardly knew what to say. Give up his vineyard — he couldn't do that! " I cannot let you have this vineyard, O King," he said. " God forbid that I give up what I have inherited from my family."

The king went away very angry. He was determined to get that vineyard!

Then Ahab's wife said, " Come now, be cheerful and eat your food. I will get the vineyard for you! Remember that you are the king, and you should have anything you want."

The king knew that the only way his wife could get the vineyard was by doing some wrong to Naboth. But he did nothing to stop her. He wanted that vineyard!

The queen wrote letters to the rulers of the city and stamped them with the king's private seal. " Take Naboth and place him before all the people. Get two wicked men to come and say that he has cursed God and said evil things about the king. When everyone gets angry with Naboth, take him out and stone him to death."

The city rulers were afraid not to obey the queen, especially when the letters had the king's own seal on them. Naboth protested that the wicked men were telling lies about him, but the rulers pretended not to hear and the people refused to listen. They killed Naboth.

The queen could hardly wait to tell Ahab the good news. " Go and take the vineyard. Naboth is dead, and there is no one to stop you."

Before the king had time to enjoy his new vineyard, the prophet Elijah arrived to speak for God. Many times before, he had risked his life to bring God's message to the king. " You know you have done wrong, Ahab. God will surely punish you," said Elijah.

The king knew that Elijah was right. Lying, cheating, killing — what sort of king was he to think that Naboth had no rights? Ahab took off his rich robes and put on clothing of coarse, rough cloth. He went about not daring to look anyone in the eye. Everyone knew that the great and powerful ruler had done wrong and God had told him so.

Now the queen hated Elijah more than she had before. She could not understand all that was happening. Ahab was king in Israel. He had the vineyard he wanted so much. But he was the unhappiest person in all the land!

Yes, Ahab was the king, but God was still the ruler in Israel! (You can read more of this story in I Kings, chapter 21.)

A PRAYER / *Dear God, we thank you that no ruler is more powerful than you, even when he seems to get his own way. Help us to trust in your love and power, and to understand how you want us to show our love for you. Thank you for telling us when we do wrong, and forgiving us when we are sorry and want to change our ways. Amen.*

Whom Do You Trust?

HAVE YOU EVER HEARD SOMEONE SAY, " WHAT YOU DO speaks so loudly I can't hear what you say "? Do you know what the person means? It is very easy to talk about believing in something, but it is not always easy to act as though you believe it.

Long ago God, through his prophet Isaiah, spoke words with much the same meaning. The Hebrew people were living in a time of war and revolts, when kings were being defeated and their kingdoms overrun by their enemies. God's people had not been spared the evil of those dark days. Sometimes they thought that God had forgotten all about them, and left them to the mercy of those whose armies were stronger than their own. Even the rulers were frightened about what would become of their nation.

Time after time God had called the people to trust him, obey his commands, and believe in his promise to save them. His prophets reminded everyone that God had never yet failed them. The priests led them in praising and thanking God for his strength, which was the only thing to save them. There was much talk everywhere about putting their trust in God instead of in armies.

All the while, however, the Hebrew leaders were working hard to make secret pacts with this nation or that one, trying to join forces with one enemy to get their protection against another. The Hebrews became almost a slave nation in order to try to buy off one powerful attacker. They even took the silver from the Temple and the treasures from the king's own house to pay an enemy ruler to let them alone. They did not *really* trust God at all!

Isaiah called on the people to listen and obey God's word. Instead, they tried to hide from the Lord their plans and dealings with military powers that *might* help to protect them. Of course, God knew exactly what was going on. " This people draw near with their mouth and honor me with their lips, while their hearts are far from me, and their fear of me is a commandment of men learned by rote [repetition]." (Isaiah 29:13.) The prophet pointed out that if

they truly believed in God, as they said, they would stop looking for powerful friends. Instead, they would live quietly and without fear, leaving the fate of their enemies to God. They should act as they talked!

This was not easy for the Hebrew people. It does not seem very easy for us today. Even though the Bible tells how God was faithful time and time again, people cannot understand that *no* enemy is too big or too strong for God to handle. We cannot believe that our own ideas and plans might not be just a little bit better than God's. It is great to talk of trusting God, and to speak well of his faithfulness, but *just in case* he might fail this time . . . maybe it would be a good idea to follow your own plan!

Have you ever felt like this? Have you ever thought that perhaps you know a little more about the problems you have to face than God does, so maybe you should handle it in your own way? Do you need to be reminded to make your actions speak the same thing that your words are saying?

(You can read more of God's word to his impatient people in Isaiah 30:15-18.)

A PRAYER / *Dear God, forgive us for saying that we trust you, and then going about our own plans in our own way without giving any thought to your words. Help us to trust and obey you, and to act as we say we believe. Thank you for your words that tell us of your faithfulness to your people always. Thank you for Jesus, who more than anyone shows us the power of your love. Amen.*

God's Strange Ways

THE BIBLE TELLS US OVER AND OVER AGAIN OF HOW GOD works among his people to protect and care for them. Do you remember a story about a young man named Joseph whose father loved him so much that he gave him a beautiful coat? We sometimes call it " the coat of many colors." Sometimes we remember about the coat, but forget why the story is in our Bible. Read it in Genesis 37:2-4 and see if you can discover what happened because Joseph received the special coat from his father.

The story of what happened after that is a long one. You might like to read parts of it whenever you have time, and see what it tells of God's plan of caring for his people. If you do not have time to read all of it, here is part of the story in words that are easy to understand.

Joseph was the youngest of twelve boys in the family of a Hebrew leader named Jacob, and his father's favorite. One day Jacob gave to Joseph a beautiful new coat that was as fine as those worn by the chiefs of the tribes. His brothers had only their short, dull-colored shepherd's coats. Can you imagine how they felt? They were jealous and angry with this young brother who was always getting better treatment than they were. To make matters even worse, Joseph had strange dreams in which others were always bowing down before him. Instead of keeping his dreams to himself, he told his family about them. This made his brothers angrier, and they were determined to get even with him one way or another.

One day in a field a long way from home, the brothers found their chance. Joseph had come out to see if all was well with the flocks. When he came near, the brothers grabbed him and threw him into a pit that had once held water. While eating their lunch, they saw a group of merchants riding along on their loaded camels. That gave them an idea. " Let's ask these men to buy Joseph and take him along to Egypt and sell him as a slave," they said. " Then we'll tell Father that a wild animal must have killed him. We'll put blood on his coat and show it to Jacob so that he will believe us. We can be rid of Joseph forever! "

The merchants agreed to the bargain and the brothers carried out their plan. Joseph was sold in Egypt to an officer of the king. The boy worked hard, and whatever he did always seemed to turn out so well that the officer put him in charge of his house, his lands, and everything that he had. Joseph continued to be interested in dreams, and soon had a reputation for being able to tell people what their dreams meant. Even the ruler of all Egypt sent for him to tell what his dreams meant.

Joseph told the ruler that a time of poor crops would come, and that he should begin at once to store up food while there was plenty on hand. Immediately the ruler put Joseph in charge of the project.

Joseph traveled about, gathering up extra food and storing it. He did this year after year until the time came when the crops were poor and there was not enough food for everyone. Then Joseph opened the storehouses and gave the people grain.

Back in the land where Joseph's father and brothers lived, the crops were as poor as they were in Egypt. " I have heard that there is grain for sale in Egypt," said Jacob to his sons. " Go down and buy some, or we will all starve to death."

All these years old Jacob had thought his son Joseph was dead. The brothers had no idea where he had been taken. Can you imagine their surprise when they found that the man from whom they were buying grain was their own brother Joseph? He forgave them for what they had done to him, sold them grain, and ordered them to bring his father and all their families to live with him in Egypt.

Soon the family was together once again, living in peace and plenty. The ruler of Egypt gave them rich pasture-lands, where they raised their flocks and herds. The family continued to grow larger and stronger. God's promise that he would make them to become a great people seemed to be coming true.

Think about this story. How many times in it does God's

way seem to be going wrong? Joseph angered his brothers; they got rid of him; he was a slave in a foreign land; famine threatened his life; he was separated from his family. God was able to use even these events to keep the promise that he had made to this family long before. Joseph's coat may have started a large part of his trouble, but God is never prevented from fulfilling his plan for his people. That is just as true for us today as it was for Joseph so very long ago.

A PRAYER / *Thank you, God, for stories that tell us of your love and care. Thank you that nothing can keep you from doing what you promise to do for us. Thank you for Jesus, who was willing to give his life to show us that your way of love wins out over every evil and selfish way. Amen.*

The Biggest of All

ONCE THERE WAS A BOY WHO HAD A FUNNY KIND OF HOBBY. He collected lists of the " biggest " of everything he could think of! He had a list of the five highest mountains in the whole world . . . a list of the five biggest ships in the United States Navy . . . the names of the largest countries . . . the biggest cities . . . the tallest buildings . . . the heaviest trucks . . . the highest batting averages.

Sometimes he had to look and look in history books, encyclopedias, maps, and the dictionary to find out what was the very biggest something or other. And sometimes the second biggest was so close to being the really biggest that people were still arguing over which was which!

Do you know that you have a very important " biggest " that everyone else can also have as their " biggest "? Can you guess what it is? It is the love that God gives to you and to me and to every one of his people. His love is so " big " that there is enough for everyone in the whole universe —

and still there will always be more. Sometimes it seems as though God's love is " too big," when he pours it out for those who do not seem to want it. But that's because it is God's love and not man's love, and God's ways are not man's ways when it comes to showing love toward his people.

The boy who collected " biggest " lists could tell you exactly how high, or deep, or wide, or how many stories each one of the things measured. No one has ever been able to measure God's love, or to say, " God's love is *this* big, or *this* great, and no more." No one knows exactly how wide or deep or high God's love reaches. But anyone who wants to know and believe in God's love can be sure that it goes beyond any measurements that man knows. There is always more than enough love for all man's needs.

Do you know that the Bible is filled with stories about people who learned about how great God's love is? That's the most important part of the whole book. God's love is so great that he sent his only Son to tell people about it and show them how to love each other.

God loves each one of us with this same great love that we read of in the Bible. He loves *you* with that love — no matter what happens to you, or what you do, or how hard it is for you to understand about his kind of love.

Have you ever listened to your minister in church talking about Jesus, and about how he was put to death by men who could not understand who he really was or what he had come to teach them? Have you ever wondered how Jesus could have been put to death, and still be alive and with God's people? These questions show us one way to measure God's love. He is so great that he could make sure that his only Son would win out over death, even though you and I cannot understand exactly how it all happened.

If you can believe that God's love is so great that it is bigger than any measuring stick you or I or anyone else knows about, maybe you can believe that it is big enough so that nothing we do can make God say, " I do not love you."

That is the *biggest* and greatest love in the whole world.

Read in your Bible the words of John 15:9-17 and think what they tell you about God's great love for us.

A PRAYER / *Dear God, thank you for sending Jesus to make known to all of us your great love. Thank you that we can be sure there will always be more than enough love for all your people. Help us to try to love others as Jesus teaches us, and to show our love for you in all that we say and do. Thank you that your love forgives us when we make mistakes and do what we know is wrong and unloving. Amen.*

"It Makes for Confidence"

" FOUR DOLLARS AND SIXTY CENTS, PLUS TWO DOLLARS AND forty-three cents . . . plus tax . . . take away fifty cents for my allowance . . ." Dave shook his head and started to add all over again. " Stuff for an electric train sure takes a lot of money," he mumbled.

" You need a good moneymaking project," said Jamie. " Why don't you think one up? "

" Got any great ideas? " asked Dave, looking up from his paper. " Don't answer! If you did, you'd keep it to yourself. You don't have any money either."

Jamie groaned. " I sure don't. My allowance doesn't last even half the week. Racing cars take money too, remember."

The next morning Dave was still trying to think up a project. How he did need some money! As he was eating his breakfast, and staring out of the window, suddenly — he had it! A project! Hanging on the back porch of the house across the alley was a neat wooden sign on which had been painted the house number. On the *back* porch!

All the delivery trucks came down the alley, and all the deliveries were made to the back doors, for there was no parking on the busy street out in front. How many times had someone come to the door asking, " Is this 846? " Now that the back porches on Dave's side of the alley had all been rebuilt, they looked exactly alike. Everyone was complaining

because no one could find the right house anymore.

"Mother!" shouted Dave, forgetting all about breakfast. "Would you buy a sign to hang on our back porch if I made one with our house number on it?"

"I certainly would," said Mother. "Someone is always coming to our door looking for some other house."

That afternoon Dave found pieces of scrap lumber in the basement. He sawed boards into pieces big enough for signs and varnished them for protection against the weather. Then he went to the hardware store and brought black wrought-iron numbers, which he carefully nailed onto the pieces of wood. When his first sign was ready, he showed it to his mother: "850" in beautiful black numbers on the light-colored wood.

With his " 850 " sign as a sample, Dave went around the neighborhood taking orders. His price was fair, the workmanship was good, and he soon had as many orders as he could handle. At one house the lady promised to buy a sign if Dave would put it up for her on her porch.

" I'll come on Friday afternoon and put it up for you," said Dave.

On that Friday, Dave came home from school. A cold wind was blowing and snow was beginning to fall. There were fresh cookies coming out of the oven! A new television show was beginning. What a day to stay inside! But he had promised to put up a house sign!

Dave put on his heavy coat, borrowed his mother's driving gloves, took the sign, and went off to the lady's house. When she opened the door, she said, " Oh, Dave! You shouldn't have come on such a cold day. I could have waited to have my sign put up."

Dave looked at her, and at the sign, and said, " I'll put it up today, as I promised. When you say you'll do something, you should do it. That makes for confidence! "

Dave had learned something very important. He knew that if he wanted people to trust him, and have confidence in him, he would have to keep his promises to them. What words would you use to describe a boy like this?

There is a word that is often found in the Bible that tells something of Dave's determination to keep his promise. The word describes the way God acts toward his people in keeping the promises he has made about loving and caring for us. Read Psalm 100 and try to find the word. It is in the very last sentence. There are other words there that describe God's love, also. Talk about them with your family so that you may understand them better.

The whole story of the Bible tells how God acts faithfully and with steadfast love, even when his people break their promises to him. God is faithful in all his ways. God always keeps his promises. This makes for confidence!

A PRAYER / *Thank you, God, that we can trust you always. Teach us to be faithful followers of Jesus and his way of love. Help us to keep our promises to you, and to each other, so that we will be trustworthy. Teach us to show our love for others. Amen.*

85

God's Faithful Man

God
and
His
People

ONE OF THE MOST SURPRISING STORIES IN THE WHOLE Bible is about a man named Abraham. You can read about him in the book named Genesis. At first it may seem to you as though the whole story is about this man, his family, and his business affairs. Abraham, the great chieftain of a tribe of shepherd people, successfully leads them far across the desert lands to find a new home for themselves, and new pastures for their flocks and herds.

If you read the story carefully, however, you will soon find that it is God and not Abraham who is the *most* important character. It is because Abraham listened to God and trusted him, and because God was always faithful in keeping his promises to Abraham, that the story is told at all.

If this story in Genesis is only a record of what one very brave and strong old tribal chieftain did many, many years ago, then it would be a good story — and that's all. But because it is a way God has of telling those who trust him that he is faithful, it is an important story for all of us to know. And because it is also a way of telling us that God always keeps his promises to his faithful people, it is important that we understand the story.

Here are some of the ways the story tells us these things. God promised Abraham that he would make him the father of a great nation, and that through him all the nations of the earth would be blessed. Then God commanded Abraham to travel to a new land where he and his people were to make a new home for themselves. It would certainly have been far easier for Abraham to stay right where he was instead of starting off on a long trip without even knowing exactly where he was to go. After all, his people were well settled and prosperous!

Nevertheless, Abraham obeyed. He gathered together the people of the tribe with all their possessions, and they started off to an unknown land. God protected Abraham and his people in all their journeying. He guided them to fertile lands and good pastures. He gave Abraham strength to deal wisely with problems that arose among the members of the tribe. And finally, long after Abraham and Sarah, his wife, thought that they were much too old ever to have a family of their own, they became the parents of a baby boy.

All these events took place because Abraham trusted God even when he could not understand how God was going to be able to keep his promises. Over and over again, God tells us that he is faithful and wise, and that he wants his people to trust and obey him. Beginning with stories like this one about Abraham in the Old Testament, God shows himself faithful in keeping all his promises. He shows himself loving his people with a love that is stronger than any enemy man knows. God also shows us that he expects those who love him to trust him and follow his way.

When God commanded Abraham to leave home and travel far away to an unknown place, Abraham had to make a choice. All along the way he had to make more choices. But each time he had only one question to answer: Shall I trust God and follow his way, or shall I do things my own way?

Abraham trusted God and obeyed his commands. He became the father of the Hebrew nation, just as God had promised. But Abraham could have thought things over, decided to stay comfortably at home, and we probably never would have heard any such story as this about him.

There comes a time when each one of you must make this same choice for yourself — to trust God's loving care and

follow his way, or to decide to be your own boss and be satisfied with what comes of depending on your own selfishness and strength alone. God refuses to force any of his people to decide to be faithful followers. He leaves the free choice to each of us. But he never stops reminding us and showing us how loving, wise, and strong he always has been and always will be. He continues to keep his promises forever and ever.

Read together with your family Psalm 105:1-11. In these words the writer of the psalm is reminding the people of God's faithfulness to Abraham. You might like to learn the words, " Let the hearts of those who seek the Lord rejoice! "

A PRAYER / *Dear God, thank you for wanting us to love you and follow your way of love. Thank you for all the people who help us to know that you are our faithful God. Thank you most of all for Jesus, who makes known your love in a way that no one could ever do before. Help us to be your faithful followers always. Amen.*

Who Makes the Rules?

HAVE YOU EVER WISHED THAT YOU COULD BE THE ONE IN your house who could tell everyone else what to do? Have you ever thought that maybe you knew better than your mother or father what you should do about some things? Have you ever wondered just why it is that grown-ups who care about their children make so many rules about everything?

Parents who take care of their children, doctors and nurses who care for the sick and injured, all kinds of people who take care of us are part of God's plan for his world. Sometimes, however, it is hard to understand that we must follow some rules or directions that these people make to guide us.

It has always been hard for God's people to trust him enough so that they would go ahead and do what he tells them. Once long ago, when the Hebrews had been led out of the life of slavery in Egypt and had gone safely across the Red Sea to escape the soldiers chasing them, they found themselves wandering in a desert where there was no food for them to eat. Moses was their leader, so they began to complain to him that God had deserted them and they would surely starve to death. It would have been better to have stayed in Egypt!

Moses knew that God had not brought the people all this way only to leave them to die of starvation here in the wilderness. He called on God for help, and God said, " I will send bread from heaven for you."

Sure enough, the next morning when the people woke up, there on the ground was something that looked like little white flakes of snow. They had never seen anything like this before! It must be the bread that God had promised to send like rain from heaven!

Moses directed the people to gather as much as they needed of the food, which later came to be called " manna." " God has promised to send us a fresh supply every morning," said Moses. " Therefore, take only enough for one day at a time, for the food will not keep overnight."

Soon everyone was busy gathering the food. The women must have tried many ways of cooking it. The children especially enjoyed its sweet taste. And then, what do you think happened? How would you feel if you had been worrying about not having anything to eat, and then suddenly found the ground covered with food? What would you do if someone told you to gather *only enough for one day* — that there would be more tomorrow?

You have guessed what happened, haven't you? Some peo-

ple decided that it would be a shame to waste the food, so they gathered enough to last two or three days — just in case! Probably some said that it would be better to get a supply on hand and not have to go out every morning to gather more. Others may have used the excuse that they wanted to cook up a big batch at one time. You can think of other reasons for wanting more than one day's supply. Down underneath all the reasons was this: the people could not *really* trust God's promise that he would send fresh food every day!

When those who had gathered extra manna went to use it the next day, it had spoiled! It was no good at all. But there on the ground was a fresh supply, just as God had promised. On the sixth day of the week, the people were told to gather enough food for two days, so that they would not have to go out for it on the Sabbath, which was the day of rest. Once again some refused to listen. Why spend time collecting two days' supply when the manna had been coming fresh every morning? It had always spoiled before when they tried to keep it overnight.

On the morning of the seventh day, there was no manna on the ground. However, the food that had been kept overnight by the people who had gathered a two days' supply was fresh and sweet. On the Sabbath, God would send no manna. The people had been warned, and now they could go hungry for a day! This might teach them a lesson!

What do you suppose God wanted his people to learn from this experience? There are two lessons that are as important for us today as they were for the Hebrews in the desert long ago. God wants his people to trust him, even though all his reasons for doing things his way are not always clear to us. No one knows why the extra manna spoiled all week long, and then kept fresh for use on the Sabbath. We do know that people who trusted God and obeyed him had plenty of food when they needed it. We can learn from this that God keeps his promises and deserves our trust, even

when we do not understand his ways.

We can also learn that God expects his people to obey
him. The Sabbath was to be kept as the Lord's Day, and
everyone was to rest according to the laws by which the people lived as God's people. When they insisted on disobeying
him, they had to take the consequences that God had warned
them would come. This is true today, just as it was in the
time of the Hebrews.

This story seems to have little to do with our needs and
the way we live today — until we stop to listen to what it
teaches us about God's dealings with his people. Then we
hear him saying to *all* men, " Trust and obey me, for I am
your loving and faithful God." It is because God loves us
that he makes rules for us to live by, and gives us directions
for following in his way of love. If he did not care about us,
it would not matter whether we learned to trust and obey
him. We would be left on our own instead of being so caught
up in his love that he will never let us go so far away that
his love cannot bring us back to him.

(You can read more of the story of the Hebrew people
and their efforts to live as God's people in Exodus, chapter
16.)

A PRAYER / *We give thinks, O God, that you have loved us so much that you are telling us in many ways of your faithful love. Help us to hear your words speaking to us through the stories of the people of God who lived long ago. Help us to know Jesus and to learn from him the greatness of your love and forgiveness, so that we can be faithful followers of your way. Amen.*

The Ancient Paths

MARY CAME RUNNING ALONG THE SIDEWALK, UP THE FRONT steps, and burst into the house all out of breath. " Here I am, Mother," she called. " Is Aunt Ruth here yet? "

There was no answer! That was strange, because Mary was supposed to meet Aunt Ruth at two P.M. sharp! Where could Mother be? Where was Aunt Ruth?

Just then Mary saw a note on the bulletin board beside the telephone. It said, *" Mary, come next door. Mother."*

Mary dashed out and across the driveway to the Fishers' house. Her mother was watching from the window and opened the door. " Mary, where have you been? " she said.

Mary looked down at her shoes, fixed her belt buckle, and swallowed hard. " I went to Rick's house and his mother was making cookies. She said we could have some as soon as they were baked. I guess maybe that took a little longer than — Mother, is Aunt Ruth waiting for me somewhere else? "

Mother looked very serious. " Come and sit down, Mary," she said. " Speak softly, because the baby has just gone to sleep. He's been sick, you know, and that's why I had to come over here. I promised Mrs. Fisher I would sit with him while she goes to the drugstore and to the market."

Mary sat down beside her mother. Oh, what if I'm too late? she thought. But that was *too* awful! It couldn't be! Aunt Ruth was going to take her on the sight-seeing bus to the zoo to see the new twin bear cubs. And because she had

worked there, Aunt Ruth had permission to take Mary back to the feeding room and see lots of things one could never see otherwise. Mary had been counting on this trip for weeks! She had even bragged to the girls at school about how she could go places they were not allowed to go! Maybe Aunt Ruth was late!

Mother was talking. " You promised faithfully that you would be home by half past one, Mary. Aunt Ruth told you that if you missed the two o'clock bus, there was not another one until three o'clock, and that would get you to the zoo too late for feeding time. She had made all these special arrangements because she is doing some work at school and wanted to take pictures of the little cubs being fed. I'm sorry, Mary, but Aunt Ruth came and waited as long as she could. Then she had to go on to the zoo alone."

Mary wanted to cry. No trip, no bear cubs, no nothing. The day was ruined. Mary *did* cry. " Why do such mean things have to happen to me? " she sobbed. " I couldn't help it if I forgot. Oh, I hate everybody! "

Mother waited until the sobs had stopped. Then she said quietly, " There's one thing we all have to learn, dear. If we insist on not keeping our promises, and make excuses for not doing what we know should be done, we have to suffer the results. Sometimes it's a hard lesson, like this one for you. Sometimes one hard lesson is enough to teach us not to re- peat the same mistake again. I hope you get another chance to see the bear cubs, Mary. If you do, I'm sure you will not miss it by being late."

Long ago, the prophet Jeremiah reminded the Hebrew people of God's laws which he had commanded them to obey. The prophet called them " ancient paths," because they were laws given by God long before as guides or ways the people were to follow. When they chose some other way instead, trouble was always the result. The " good way " was the one in which people lived when they followed the " ancient paths." Read the verse in Jeremiah 6:16 and think how it could help you to walk in God's " good way."

A PRAYER / *Dear God, we thank you for the " ancient paths " you have given us for traveling in your way of love. Help us to understand how to walk in your way today, to show our love toward you and toward all your people, and to keep the promises we make about wanting to be your children. Thank you for forgiving us when we decide to go our own way instead of yours. Thank you for your love that is still with us even when we are on the way that is not your " good way." Amen.*

A God with Big Ears

NATHAN AND AMUR SAT ON THE BANK OF THE CANAL WITH their feet splashing in the warm water. They had raced each other from the village where Nathan's family lived, and now it was good to rest and watch the boats coming and going on the canal. People from everywhere came to Babylon to trade and to bring the news of wars in places near and far away. It was an exciting place to live! Nathan could not remember ever living anywhere else.

Amur pulled from his pocket a little statue which he held out to Nathan. " See what my grandfather gave me for a present? It's Marduk, the greatest god of all. He will protect me if I carry this in my pocket and if I don't forget to leave a sacrifice for him in front of the big statue in our house."

"Let's see," said Nathan, and he took the tiny statue into his own hand. "He looks funny to me," he said. "What's the matter with his head?'"

Quickly Amur snatched the statue and hid it in his pocket. His eyes were dark with anger. Or was it fear? "Don't talk like that about Marduk," he said. "He'll hear you."

Nathan looked puzzled. "I didn't say anything bad about him," he said. "I just asked why his head looks . . . well, different."

Amur cautiously took the statue out of his pocket again. "It's his ears!" he said. "See, they are almost as big as his whole head. That's why Marduk can hear *everything,* Nathan. He knows absolutely every single thing that goes on. He's the greatest god there is. Marduk can do anything. I'm going to keep this statue with me forever, and then I'll always be able to pray right to him!"

That night Nathan told his father about the little statue. "Why can't I carry a statue of our one true God, Father?" he said. "I could carve one out of wood, and then I would always have him with me, the way Amur does with Marduk."

Nathan's father looked very stern. "My son," he said, "no one can make a statue of our God, because no one knows what he looks like. No one has seen him — that is, to know about his ears or his eyes or anything like that. Our God is too great for any man to even imagine what he looks like."

"Couldn't I just make a pretend statue, then, so I could show Amur that we worship God? He's always asking me where our God is!" said Nathan.

Father banged his fist on the table. " Don't ever let me find you carrying any statues of anyone, Nathan," he said. " It is because some of our people insisted on worshiping other gods, just like the one Amur showed you today, that we are living here in Babylon as captive people. God warned us that if we did not obey his commands and trust him, we would be driven from our homes and our Temple would be destroyed. That is exactly what happened. God said, ' You shall have no other gods before me. . . . You shall not worship images that you make of any gods.' Our people would not listen. They trusted in armies and foreign gods to save us. Now you see what has happened. Here we are, and who knows when we will ever get back home again."

Nathan had never seen his father so angry. But he decided to risk one more question. " How do we know God hasn't left us here alone? " he asked. " How do we know we even have a God, so far away from home? Amur can *see* his god, and talk to him — right to him! He has the biggest ears you ever saw! " And Nathan laughed to remember the look of the little statue.

Father's voice was always quiet when he was going to say a *most important* something! " Our God has promised to be with us always. He has never broken his promise, Nathan — never! He only asks us to trust him. God has promised that someday the people who are faithful to him will go back to Jerusalem, our home. We must trust him that he is with us here in Babylon, and that he is greater than all these strange gods — even greater than Marduk. We can read his promise in the laws and writings of our people; we know what he has done in the past; we must trust his word that he will never go away and leave us."

Nathan was still a little puzzled. " But I *know* my father is right," he said. " I don't understand all about it, but I *know* God is here even if I don't have his statue to carry around. Maybe someday I'll know more about it. Maybe I will be one of those who go back to Jerusalem! "

Do you wonder how this story might have ended? It is a story about make-believe people, but you will find the events told in the Bible. God's people were set free by the conqueror Cyrus, and they went back to Jerusalem to rebuild their city. Nathan and his father may have heard their leaders say to them the words you can read in Isaiah 41:10. When you wish sometimes that you could see God, or touch him, or hear him speak as you hear your friends, remember this verse and know that God truly is with his people. Our God is too great to be made into a little good-luck piece to be carried around in a pocket!

A PRAYER / *Dear God, thank you for being too great for us to put into our pockets! Help us to keep you in our hearts instead. Amen.*

Start Where You Are!

HAVE YOU EVER MADE A NEW YEAR'S RESOLUTION? HOW long did you remember to keep it? Maybe you tried very hard for a while to be more friendly and kind, to be more helpful at home, or to do your work to the best of your ability. Then, if you are like most people, you forgot once — and then again — and again. By this time you were discouraged and decided to forget the whole thing! You could always try again next year.

New Year's resolutions are fun, and not really terribly important. However, the way we excuse ourselves from keeping them *is* important. It is easy to get into the habit of thinking, " Oh, well, I forgot again. I'll try to do better some other time." Or perhaps you begin to feel as though you can never live up to what you know is right, or be the person God intends you to be. What's the use trying when you know you will never be like that!

There is a story in Genesis, chapter 13, that tells how two rich and powerful men settled a dispute over which part of the new land that God had given them each one would claim as his own. We learn how the men went out together to look over the country. The older one, Abraham, said to his nephew, Lot, "Look around and take whichever section of the land you want. I will take the other and be satisfied. Then there will be no more fighting among our herdsmen, and we can live in peace together."

Lot chose the fertile river valley, leaving the land called Canaan to his uncle Abraham. Think how the older man may have felt. His nephew had come with him on the long trip to this new land. Abraham was the one chosen by God to lead the tribe on their journey. He was the one who had made the decisions, obeyed and trusted God, and brought everyone safely to their new home. Now Lot had chosen first, and it seemed as though he had chosen the better part of the land. Perhaps the trip had been for nothing, so far as Abraham was concerned. Maybe this leftover piece of the country would be no better than what he had left behind him. God had promised to make Abraham the father of a great nation, but he did not even have a son of his own. How could there come a nation from his family?

You can read in Genesis 13:14-15 what God said to Abraham. After you have read the words in your Bible, think of this way of saying them, as another translator has done: "Raise your eyes now. . . . Look from the place where you are . . ." (American Standard Version.)

The only way to begin to do anything is to start from where you are. It does no good to feel sorry for yourself, or to make excuses for past failures, or to say that you cannot do better. God does not wait until you achieve a certain degree of "goodness" before he is interested in helping you. God wants to be with you and start with you from wherever you are. God wants you to "raise your eyes," not up to some faraway goal that you may never be able to reach, but to him

— looking to his love and strength to help you as he has promised that he will do for all his people if they will turn to him.

What Abraham was to do with the remaining years of his life was important to God. Therefore, he urged Abraham to look up to him and find strength to do the work that God intended for him. What you do with your life is equally important to God. He is calling you, too, to look up to him and

RESILUSHONS.
I WILL MAKE
MY BED AND
I WILL KEPE MY
ROOM TIDY WHEN
I WANT
TO
ANIM

count on his love and strength to make your life what he intends it to be.

Why not take a clue from the title of a television program you may have seen at one time — "Look Up and Live"?

A PRAYER / *We will lift up our eyes to our God, from whom comes strength for each day's living. We praise thee, O God, for all the promises you have made to your people, to care for and love us. We give thanks that you are our faithful God, whose love never fails. Amen.*

Love Is a Risk

ROBBIE CAME HOME FROM SCHOOL, THREW HIS BOOKS ON the table, and called, "Mother! Where are you?" There was no answer. Robbie went into the kitchen and checked the blackboard where Mother always left notes and instructions for everyone. There was a note marked "Robbie." He opened it and read, "Go to Mrs. Benton's house right away. Love, Mother."

Mrs. Benton's house — that was strange. Mr. Benton was their minister. Why should he go there? But Robbie started off, still wondering why he should go to Mrs. Benton's.

Both Mr. and Mrs. Benton were waiting for him at the door. "Come in, Robbie. We've been waiting for you. Your mother said she would leave you a note. Sit here with me, because I have something to tell you."

Robbie was more puzzled than ever. Something must be wrong! Where was his mother?

Before he could ask any questions, Mr. Benton said, "Robbie, your father was hurt today in an accident in the plant where he works. He is in the hospital, and has good doctors taking care of him. We do not know how badly he is injured. Your mother is there with him. She wanted me to tell you all about it, and to answer all your questions if I can.

You are not to keep back anything you want to ask, because your mother said to tell you that she is counting on you to come through this with her."

At first Robbie could not think of anything to say. It didn't seem real. Maybe it was just a story or something! Or perhaps it was just a little bit of an accident after all. Then the questions began to pour out. " How did it happen? " " Where is Daddy hurt? " " How long will he be in the hospital? " " When will my mother be home ?" " Who will take care of me? " " What can I do to help my daddy? "

The Bentons answered every question as well as they could. Then Mr. Benton said, " I am going to the hospital to bring your mother here to stay with us tonight. You will stay, too. Tomorrow you can decide together how you will manage things. Before I go, let's pray for your family."

Mr. Benton prayed, " Dear God, who loves us all more

than we know, help Robbie and his mother and daddy in a special way today. Help the doctors to be skillful and to know what is best to do to make Robbie's daddy well again. Help Robbie and his mother to trust your love, and allow you to give them strength and comfort while they are troubled about the person they love so much. Give Robbie's daddy a special measure of strength to fight to get well. May we all feel your arms holding us in your loving care. Amen."

That night Robbie had a long talk with his mother. " I do not know how long Daddy will be in the hospital," she said, " but I think that it may be a long, long time. The doctors say that someday he will be well again so that he can work, but it will take a long time for his injuries to heal. You and I must take care of each other now, Robbie. Daddy said to tell you that he is counting on you."

Robbie leaned his head on his mother's shoulder. " I wish things like this didn't happen to us," he said.

Mother put her arm around Robbie. " This is part of being a family, Robbie," she said. " We love each other so much that when one of us is hurt or unhappy, the others suffer too. That's the risk you run when you choose to love someone, dear. Loving is joy, and it is also sharing the sorrows and hurts of those you love. I know it's hard to understand, but it's true."

The next morning Robbie wrote his father a note. " Dear Daddy, I am very sorry that you got hurt. I am taking care of Mother and she is taking care of me. We want you to get well very fast. I miss you all the time. If I didn't love you so much, it wouldn't hurt so bad! Love, Robbie."

It is part of God's plan that people should live together in families, loving each other and caring for each other in special ways. This kind of love means that we run the risk of getting hurt, because the more we love someone, the more we feel the hurts and troubles that come to him. Have you ever heard your parents say, " I wish I could be sick instead of you. It wouldn't hurt as much as seeing you suffer "?

There is a special kind of comfort that comes to families when trouble or sadness is faced together. One person comforts another, and God's love is often felt in a way that they have never known before. No one can explain this, or even describe it. You have to feel it to know what it is all about. Love is a risk . . . and God's love is what gives us courage to run the risk of being hurt when those we love must suffer.

A PRAYER / *Dear God, thank you for our families, and for the love and care we show to one another. When troubles come, help us to have courage as together we show our love even while we are feeling sad or lonely or sorry for the one who is sick or in pain. Thank you that your love is with us in a special way at times like this. Amen.*

God Doesn't Listen!

BETSY AND CARL EACH HAD TWENTY-FIVE CENTS THAT they had earned by delivering notices of a neighborhood meeting to all the houses in their block. They had decided to put their money together and buy a kite. " We can take turns flying it," they said. " It would be better to buy one kite together than to wait until we could earn this much more money."

They went to the store and found the counter where the kites were on display. The sign said, KITES — 50¢ EACH. Besty looked at her money and Carl looked at his money. Together it made fifty cents.

" We would like to buy a kite, please," said Betsy.

" Do you have the money? " asked the salesgirl.

" I have twenty-five cents," said Betsy.

" And I have . . ." began Carl. But the salesgirl wasn't listening. " Kites are fifty cents, little girl. You don't have enough money." And she was walking away to take care of another customer.

"I have some money, too," called Carl. The salesgirl only shook her head and waved at them to go away and not bother her.

When the children got home, Carl went to look for his father. "Daddy! Where are you? Will you help us buy a kite?" he called.

Daddy was busy down in the basement. "I think you have spent enough money this week, Carl. You'll have to buy it with your own money if you want a kite."

"But, Daddy, I *have* the money . . . or Betsy and I do together," said Carl.

"Don't keep on pestering," called Daddy. "I'm very busy right now. You know what I said about giving you more money."

Carl looked at Betsy. "Just like that girl in the store! He won't listen!"

That night when Betsy was saying her prayers, she stopped suddenly. " What's the matter? " asked Mother. " You did not finish your prayers."

" Maybe I won't finish at all," said Betsy. " If God is like that girl in the store or like Daddy when he's busy in the basement, what's the use of praying. Maybe God won't listen either! "

After Mother heard all of the story, she said, " Grownups have a bad habit of not really listening carefully to children. Sometimes it's because we're busy. Sometimes we think we know what they are going to say before they say it — and that is wrong. But God is never too busy, and he always wants to know our thoughts and feelings. It doesn't matter how old you are when you pray to God — he listens! God wants you to come to him to give praise and thanks, to ask for his help, and to tell him whatever you want to say. Don't ever think that he is not listening, Betsy."

Mother opened the Bible and read, " ' Let the children come to me.' " Then she told Betsy how Jesus once had scolded the disciples for sending the children away for fear that they would bother him. Jesus called the children back, took them in his arms, and gave them his blessing. " ' Let the children come to me,' " read Mother again.

You may be sure that Betsy's mother was right. God calls children to him, just as he calls people of all ages. When you forget this sometimes, and think that maybe you should not bother to pray because God might not listen, remember the verse that Betsy learned. You can find it in your Bible in Mark 10:14.

A PRAYER / *Dear God, who loves little children and big people too, thank you for always listening to us when we pray. Help us to trust you, and to know that you will never send us away because you are too busy or too tired to listen to us. Thank you for your love, and for hearing and answering prayers. Amen.*

God's Surprises

LONG, LONG AGO THE HEBREW PEOPLE WERE LIVING AS captives in the land called Babylon. They had a good life and were allowed to do almost anything they wanted to do — except one thing. They were not allowed to go back home to Jerusalem.

This made the people very sad. Their Temple was in Jerusalem. That was where they could worship God. How could they worship him here in this strange land, surrounded by all sorts of gods that the Babylonians worshiped? How did they know that God was here with them? Maybe he had stayed behind in Jerusalem and had permitted them to go off all alone!

Questions like these puzzled the Hebrews and made them more unhappy all the time. Their neighbors teased them for believing in one God. " If your God is so great, why doesn't he do something for you? Why don't you try some of our gods and see if they don't have more power than your God? Look what they do for us! We would never think of putting all our trust in only one of them."

Sometimes it seemed that their Babylonian neighbors were right. Everything was right for them and wrong for the Hebrews. Babylon grew stronger and stronger, and the chances of the Hebrews' winning their freedom grew less and less. Some of the people began to keep little statues of the Babylonian gods in their homes — just in case these gods *could* do something to help them.

The religious leaders tried to think of ways that God might use to set them free. Prophets who came to speak God's word assured the people that God was here in Babylon with them, and that he wanted them to trust and obey him. If they would listen to God's word and turn from their wrong ways, he would take them back to Jerusalem. But no one could say how this would happen!

The years went by, and many of the people forgot all

about going back to their old home. Babylon was such a strong nation, she would never be defeated. Nothing would make her let the captive Hebrews go free. The only person to worry about seemed to be King Cyrus, who had been winning so many battles for his country that he might decide to attack Babylon. If that occurred, who knew what terrible things might happen to the Hebrews.

News of Cyrus and his armies became more frightening. The mighty leader was on his way to Babylon, conquering everything in his path. No one seemed to be able to stop him. Soon he was camped right outside the gates of the city. The Hebrews prayed to God to save them.

Cyrus captured the city with scarcely any fighting, for the Babylonians decided it was useless to resist his great army. Soon afterward a surprising thing happened. Heralds rode through the streets calling all the Hebrews to come to hear a message from King Cyrus. Everyone crowded close to hear what it said.

" Thus says King Cyrus," read the herald. " Those among you who are people of God are free to go back to Jerusalem and rebuild your Temple! "

Who would have thought that God would choose to use a conquering hero, whom all the world feared, as his way of setting the Hebrews free? Who but God could do such a thing? God's way is full of surprises!

God's word to his people today through stories such as this one is telling us that nothing is impossible with him. It is also reminding us that God's ways are not our ways — that his ways are often surprising. God can and does do the most amazing things when it is time for his plan to move forward and his love to be made known. The most amazing of all God's surprises is in the life and death and rising again of Jesus Christ, who shows us once and for all that absolutely *nothing* is greater than God's power and love.

A PRAYER / *Dear God, even when we do not understand all your ways, help us to trust your love and believe in your promise that you will always be with your people. Help us to learn from the Bible stories that you have always been faithful to those who trust and obey your commands to love you. Amen.*

God Is Always Ready

BECKY SQUIRMED AROUND ON THE HARD LITTLE CHAIR IN the doctor's office. There were big people in all the big chairs. Every time one of them left to go in to see Dr. King, another one came in the door! There was never a comfortable chair for Becky!

" I'm tired waiting, Mother," she said. " Why can't it be my turn now? We were here before those two boys that went in."

" I'm sorry it is taking so long, dear," Mother said. " Those boys needed something special that couldn't wait, so Dr. King had to take time to see them before he sees the rest of us out here. All the others had appointments before ours. Dr. King must have been kept at the hospital later than usual, and so he was not able to start work here on time."

Later that afternoon Mother and Becky went to the supermarket. They bought some bread and peanut butter, some fruits and vegetables, some cookies and juices, and some paper napkins and soap. They had a cart full of groceries when they went to the check-out place. There was a long line of people, all waiting to check out their purchases, too.

Becky stood on one foot, then on the other. " I'm tired of waiting, Mother," she said. " Why can't it be our turn now? "

At the dinner table that evening, Father was serving the juicy roast beef that Mother had cooked. A piece for grandmother, a piece for Mother, then some little pieces for baby Harold. " I'm tired of waiting, Father," said Becky. " Why can't it be my turn now? "

When it was bedtime, Becky's mother came to tuck her in. " Did you say your prayers, dear? " she asked.

Becky yawned. " Yes, I did. I could hardly keep awake long enough to say them, but I did. Mother, I'm glad I don't have to wait in line to pray to God! "

Mother smiled. " God is always ready to listen to his people when they pray to him," she said. " In fact, God is waiting for us to come to him. He never keeps us waiting."

A PRAYER / *Dear God, thank you for wanting us to love you and come to you with our prayers. Thank you for not making us wait for our turn. Sometimes we forget to thank you, or to tell you about our troubles. Thank you for not going away, but waiting for us to come back. Amen.*

What Kind of Judge Is God?

THE NEWSPAPERS WERE FULL OF THE STORY ABOUT A MAN who had taken a large sum of money from a bank where he worked. The man said that he had *not* taken the money . . . that there had been a big mistake. Day after day the lawyers argued, and the judge listened. Finally everyone had said all that there was to say. Now it was time for the judge to decide who was right, and what should be done about the man.

It was not easy for the judge to make up his mind. He wanted to be fair and honest. He did not want to make the wrong decision. He wanted to forgive the man if there had been a mistake. The judge took a long time to think everything over and decide what to do.

Sometimes we say that God is like a judge. God knows what is right and good for his people; he knows how they should speak and act if they are to follow his way of love. God does not have to spend a lot of time thinking things over to decide what we are doing with our lives. God is not like the judge who had trouble making up his mind about the man. God knows when we are following his commands, and when we are turning away from him to go our own way.

God is ready to forgive us before we even ask him. He is not like the judge who has to decide whether or not the man deserves to be forgiven. God wants to forgive us; he wants us to come to him and say that we have done wrong. Then he helps us to turn from that wrong way and follow his way. He does not wait until we have *proved* that we deserve his forgiveness, for we can never do that. His love and forgiveness are so great that nothing we can do will ever earn our share of his love. He is ready and waiting to give it freely.

God *does* judge us, for he has made us so that we can understand right and wrong. His first concern is not to punish us, but to love us back to himself! The punishment most often comes as a result of our own wrongdoings. It is not a punishment given to us by God. He is a judge — but one who judges in love and not in anger.

Psalm 86:5 tells what kind of judge God is:

" For thou, O Lord, art good and forgiving,
    abounding in steadfast love to all who call on thee."

A PRAYER / *O God, we call upon you to hear our prayers. We ask you to forgive us when we do what we know is not the way you want your people to speak and act. We ask you to help us to learn your way of love, and to practice it even when it is hard to do. Amen.*

Afraid to Go Home

HAVE YOU EVER THOUGHT THAT BECAUSE CERTAIN MEN and women were Bible characters, they must have been very good all the time? Have you thought that they did not have problems like yours — just because their stories are in the Bible? If your answer is yes, you are all wrong! The Bible characters were always running into trouble just because they had the same big problem that you and I have. They wanted to do things their own way! Then, when the result was trouble, they were afraid of God and of what was going to happen to them. These stories are in the Bible so that you and I

can learn from them why God's way is best, and what God does about helping people to understand this.

Once there was a man named Jacob. The Bible story tells us that he played a trick on his brother by stealing property and family rights that were not honestly his. He lied to his father, cheated his brother, and finally had to run from his home and family because he feared that they would kill him for all that he had done. Jacob seems to have done all the mean and dishonest things that a person could do!

For years Jacob was afraid to go back home. He stayed far away, and learned some hard lessons about the kind of man that God wanted him to be. Jacob was supposed to be a leader, but God was not ready to use him yet. Jacob had to learn that he could not get away or hide his ways from God. He also had to learn that God was with him, even when he did not live up to what God expected of him. Jacob finally learned that God was going to use him in spite of his failures.

This meant that Jacob had to go back home. He had to face his brother whom he had cheated. He had to risk his brother's anger. Maybe his brother would even kill him! You couldn't blame him, at that.

But if Jacob was going to be the leader of his people as he believed God intended him to be, he would have to go back and face his brother's anger. He was afraid of his brother!

Jacob was also afraid of God, who knew better than anyone else how mean and wicked he had been. What if God would not stay with him? What if God would punish him by leaving him to depend on his own strength and wisdom? Jacob was a rich man, with many servants and a large family. Nevertheless, he knew that without God he was lost before he started. He was afraid that God would desert him, and he was afraid to face his brother if God was not with him.

Jacob was also afraid of himself. He knew how he had lied and cheated and stolen to get what he wanted. He knew that he was not a " good " man who deserved God's forgiveness and help. He knew that he was not the sort of person he himself would have chosen as a leader for a great nation! But God had chosen him for some purpose of his own. How could he be sure that he could do what God wanted him to do? What if he went back to his old ways after he got back home? Jacob was afraid that he would not be able to do the job.

The story in the Bible is a long one, for it tells how Jacob thought and prayed and puzzled as he struggled over the fears and questions that would not leave him. He could not sleep at night from worrying over them. Finally, he was convinced that God would be with him and would give him strength to become the leader of his people. He trusted God, and started back to meet his brother — and to face whatever might come. Jacob was afraid to go home. Only God could give him the courage to go. If you want to know what happened when the two brothers met, you can read about it in your Bible in Genesis 33:1-11.

In this story, God is telling us that we need not be afraid to come " home " to him, even though we have done some of the worst acts one can think of. God knows us for what we are, he knows the selfish things we do, the mean thoughts we have, and how many things we cannot do. Yet he knows his plan for us, and what he can do with us if we will turn to him in trust and obedience. If we will be honest about ourselves, and allow God to give us the strength and the help that he has promised, then we need never be afraid to turn to God. We never need to try to hide from him. We should never be afraid to go " home " to God.

A PRAYER / *Dear God, thank you for stories about men, like Jacob, who are so much like ourselves. We do not like to admit our faults. We do not want to see ourselves as we really are. We are afraid to try to be the persons you want us to be. Be with us always, and give us courage to trust you and walk in your way. Thank you for being faithful and loving even when we deserve it the least. Amen.*

Hello, God!

MARCIA CRUMPLED UP THE PIECE OF PAPER ON WHICH she had been writing and threw it at the wastebasket. It missed! Several others had missed, also, because the floor around the basket was cluttered with crumpled up paper.

"Hi!" said Marcia's big brother, Bob, as he came into the room to look for his history book. "Are you going out for baseball? You'll never make a pitcher by the looks of that mess!"

"Oh, pooh!" said Marcia. "Go away. I'm writing something."

Bob kicked at the papers. "Writing? There's nothing

much on these papers." He smoothed out several sheets and read, "'A Prayer,'" "'Dear God, I . . . ,'" and "'For all the . . .'"

Marcia groaned. " We're supposed to write a prayer that sounds as though we are just talking to God. Not some long things with a lot of words like ' bless ' and ' merciful,' and stuff like that. It's supposed to be something we want to say to God. I don't know how to begin."

Bob flopped into the big chair beside his sister. " That shouldn't be too hard," he said. " Let's see. Why not think a minute about what God is like. You know, if you ask Mother for something, you just go right to her and say what you want because you know she will listen and pay attention to you."

" And if I ask that grumpy old man in the toy store something, I know he'll growl at me. So mostly I don't ask him. I get someone else to do it! " laughed Marcia.

" You get the idea," said Bob. " Now, what is God like? That comes first."

" Well," said Marcia, biting on her pencil, " I think he wants me to come to him, so I think he won't mind listening. He won't say he's too busy, or anything like that. And I can say whatever I want, because he won't get mad and stop loving me . . . I know that! So I'm not afraid. And I guess God likes to know that I am thankful and glad for things he does for us, so he wants me to tell him that."

" It sounds as though you were going to talk to an old friend! " said Bob. " Now you should think about *why* you are praying to God. Any ideas? "

" Oh, sure," said Marcia. " I want to! I wouldn't like it if I thought I couldn't pray to God especially when I need help! I guess I pray sometimes because I think I should — and sometimes because everyone else is praying, like in church or at the table or something."

" You said before that you prayed because God wanted you to," said Bob.

" U'mmm h'mmmm," said Marcia. " And because I *need* to. You can't get along on your own all the time, so you need God's help and you need to ask him."

" I think you *need* to say thank you too," said Bob. " People who never have fun saying thanks miss a lot."

" Can I write something now? " asked Marcia. " I want to get finished before I have to take my piano lesson."

" Well, think about what you have just told me. God is loving and kind and you know he is waiting to hear your prayers. You want to go to him to tell him about a lot of things. If God were someone you could see and touch, like Mother or Daddy or a favorite friend, what would you say? "

Marcia waited a minute before she answered. Then she grinned and said, " I think I'd just say, ' Hello, God! ' "

Can you finish the prayer for yourself? What kind of prayer would yours be when you thought about God as Marcia did? When you feel like saying, " Hello, God! " because you know he loves you and wants to hear your prayers, what would you say after that? You could write down some ideas and use them to say a prayer with your family. Or you might like to use this prayer as your own:

A PRAYER / *Hello, God! I want to tell you that I think the spring (or fall or summer or winter) days we are having are wonderful. Thank you for making such a beautiful world. I'd also like to say that I had a hard time today being nice to _____, and I need your help so that I can do better tomorrow. There are some things that have happened to my family that I don't understand why they should happen to us, and I just want to admit that I have a little trouble trusting that you will care for us all. But I really do trust you! I guess it's just that I'm puzzled over the way you do things. I also want to say thank you a million times for all the love I get from my mother and father, and lots of other people — and from you. Amen.*

How Far Away Is "Lost"?

" PEOPLE IN THE BIBLE ARE ALWAYS LOOKING FOR SOME-
thing that is lost," said Freddie.

" What do you mean? " asked Father. " What makes you
say that? "

Freddie pointed to the pages in the last part of the big

Bible. " Miss Winter told us about this thing where you can look up words and see where they are used in verses in the Bible. She gave us each a word to look up, and mine is ' lost.' Look how long the list is! "

" That is called a concordance," said Father. " I'm glad you are learning how to use it."

" Listen to this," said Freddie, running his finger down the page. " They lost sheep, coins, people, a son, hope, and all sorts of things! Why is there so much about losing stuff in the Bible? "

" Let me ask you a question first," said Father. " When is something lost? "

" Well, if I don't know where it is, I guess it's lost," said Freddie. " Like my bike was lost because I couldn't find it until Chuck reminded me I had left it in his garage to get the tire fixed."

" But if Chuck knew your bike was there, was it really lost? " asked Father.

Freddie looked puzzled. " I guess not lost from Chuck, but it was lost from me! I didn't know where it was."

" Then when something is lost, it is really gone from someone who cares about where it is," said Father. " Do you agree? "

" My bike was gone from me . . . and I cared! " said Freddie. " I guess I agree."

" Now then," said Father. " How far away does something have to be in order to be lost? "

" Well, it has to be where you can't see it," said Freddie. " My bike was pretty far away. But I lost my lunch money and it was in my desk at school all the time, under a pile of junk! "

" A great many of the ' lost ' items in the Bible are talking about people. The ' lost ' son had gone away from his father and lived a selfish life that made him miserable and unhappy. The story tells how his father welcomed him back home. The ' lost ' sheep are often people who go away from

God's love. They turn their backs on him and refuse to listen to his word. They are ' lost ' until they turn back to God. The ' coin ' you mentioned might have been right in the woman's own house, but as long as she could not find it, it was ' lost ' to her."

" Then I guess you don't have to be too far away to be lost," said Freddie.

" There's another interesting thing about the ' lost ' idea in the Bible," said Father. " We say that God knows where we are and all about us all the time. How can anyone be ' lost ' if God knows where the person is? "

" That's too hard to figure out," said Freddie.

" The Bible is trying to tell us that we are ' lost ' from God by our own selfishness. We want to have our own way, so we turn from God and refuse to listen or obey him. He knows *where* we are, but we refuse his love and forgiveness and are ' lost ' because we have decided to go away from these gifts instead of accepting them." Father stopped talking and looked at Freddie. " Do you get it? " he asked.

" I think so," said Freddie. " You might say that getting lost from God is only turning your back! "

" You get it," said Father.

If you have a concordance in a Bible in your house, look for the words " lose " and " lost." Then read one of the passages listed there. If you have no concordance, you might like to read the story of the " lost " son in Luke 15:11-32. Find out what happened when the son was " found." What did being " lost " and then " found " mean to the son and his father? Does this story fit Freddie's definition of " lost "?

A PRAYER / *Thank you, God, that you are not willing to allow any of us to stay " lost." Thank you for searching us out and calling us back to your loving care. Thank you for all the people and ways by which you tell us of your great love so that we will not turn our backs on you and get " lost " in our own selfish ways. Amen.*

Christmastime

III

PEOPLE RARELY ARE WILLING TO WORK, suffer, and sometimes die for anything or anyone who is not *real*. The story of the Christian church, of which you and your family are a part, is the story of men and women who believe in Jesus Christ. He is for them not some mythological character, some storybook man. He is *real*.

Christmas for the Christian is the birthday of this real Jesus, in whom God " became flesh " and dwelt among his people. Through his coming, there has been revealed as never before or since the absolute supremacy of God's love. This mighty act is the foundation of all our hopes and all our beliefs.

It is a difficult thing to maintain something of the importance of this event amid the rush of Santa Claus parties and struggle to buy gifts. At the same time, there is more talk about the holiday and more expectation of some religious association — whatever it may be! — than there is about religion at any other one time of the year. The problem for parents is how to find the moments in all the opportunities created by the holiday excitement and expectation in which to praise God for his gift of love and to search out something more of the meaning of this gift in the lives of those they love.

Because Christmastime has a kind of beginning and ending, it is sometimes easier to decide upon and keep a specific family schedule for appropriate Bible-reading and prayer. This may stretch through Advent and Christmas itself, or it may be centered in the celebration of Christmas Day. Even more valuable, however, may be the unplanned moments when families are together and children ask questions.

The following readings may provide some help to you in answering these questions and wonderings. They may also be used for reading with your family, and for suggesting other questions that you may want to explore together. Be sure to make use of the wealth of fine devotional materials to be found in the magazines and publications that will be coming into your home at this time of the year. Why not start a Family Christmas Scrapbook in which to collect the choice poems, stories, and pictures that you can use year after year?

A Blessed Christmas to you!

What Is a Holiday?

LET'S PLAY A GAME. TAKE YOUR PENCIL AND PRINT H O L I D A Y. Now draw a V above the letter I so that the bottom of the V rests on the top of the I. What new letter does it make? Read the new word H O L Y D A Y. Now draw a straight line down between the Y and the D and you will have two words, Holy Day. If you look up " holiday " in your dictionary, you will find that one of the definitions is your new word " holyday," or " holy day."

Christmas is one of the most important of all holidays for Christians everywhere because it is truly a " holy day." Your dictionary will also tell you that the word " holy " means something relating to Jesus and his life, or something sacred and worthy of reverence.

Holidays are times for remembering holy events that we want to celebrate in special ways. Sometimes we do not remember why or what we are celebrating. Then we do not truly celebrate the holy day at all.

Can you remember any " holy events " that help us celebrate Christmas as the time when God's Son came to bring
us God's love in a special way? Can you remember any stories of times when God kept his promise to love and care
for his people? There is the story about Abraham, to whom
God gave a son long after he and his wife had given up
hope of having a family, so that he could become the father
of a great nation as God had promised. There is much to
remember about God leading Abraham and his people safely
to a new home in a strange land, as God had promised he
would do.

There is the story about God's using Moses to bring the
Hebrew people out of Egypt where they were living as slaves,
into a land where they were free men. Even when the people grumbled and built themselves an idol to worship, God
did not go back on his promise to lead them to a new land.

There is the story we hear most often at Christmastime,
about the birth of Jesus in the little stable in Bethlehem,
where the shepherds came to kneel down and worship him
because he was not just another little, new baby — he was
Jesus, the Son of God. There is the part about Mary and
Joseph taking Jesus to Egypt to escape the anger of King
Herod, who was afraid that a new king had been born who
would take away his throne. Then there is the time when
Jesus lived in Nazareth, growing in wisdom and in stature
and in favor with God and with man.

We cannot stop " remembering " at this point in the story.
Jesus spent his life preaching and teaching that God's love
is freely given to all who will accept it. We remember the
ways Jesus showed his disciples and others around him that
we must act in love toward people as well as talk about loving them. We remember that Jesus was so sure of the power
of God's love that he was willing to die to prove that nothing could defeat God's plan. Then came the holy event that
we call the resurrection, which we remember every time
Christians gather to worship God and celebrate the good

news that Jesus lives and God's love will always triumph —
in life and in death.

Christmas is a happy holiday because we have so many
holy events to remember. Christmas is a time for celebrating, because we remember that the greatest gift of love
comes from God, who sent his Son on the first Christmas.

You can read about how the Hebrew people long ago felt
at their special times of remembering if you will open your
Bible to Psalm 42:4. You might like to change the words a
little and make this into a verse to use at Christmas. It could
sound something like this:

> These things I remember,
> as I celebrate Christmas:
> how I go with the crowds,
> and join in the services in our church,
> with happy celebrations and songs of thanks-
>   giving,
> many people together keeping this holy day
>   (holiday).

"I Wish"

PEGGY AND PETER WERE TIRED. THEY WERE CROSS TOO.
In fact, they were so tired and cross that their mother
stopped ironing, pushed the basket of clean clothes back
against the wall, and called the twins to come and sit with
her on the porch. Mother knew that it was a good thing to
stop trouble *before* it started!

" I wish . . . ," said Peggy.

" I wish . . . ," said Peter.

". . . that tomorrow was Christmas! " they both said.

Mother laughed. " So that's it! Too much waiting for
Christmas. I wonder, though . . . are both of you *ready*
for Christmas? "

The twins nodded their heads. " Oh, yes," said Peter. " I made up the list of things I want a long time ago. And I got a model ship for Barry, because he's giving me a snap-to-gether station for my train set. I got a couple of other things, too. Oh, I'm ready! "

" I'm ready, too," said Peggy. " I did all my shopping a week ago. All the parties are over, and we hurried up and went caroling early so everyone wouldn't be tired listening to the same old songs that every group sings."

" So now you wish that tomorrow was Christmas," said Mother. " Well, now let's see . . . *I* wish, too."

" What's your wish? " asked Peter.

" Are you wishing you will get the new sewing machine you want? " asked Peggy.

" No," answered Mother. " I wish that everyone would stop hurrying around *doing* so many things, and would take time to *think* about Christmas. I wish everyone would get himself ready to celebrate what Christmas is really all about! "

" But Christmas is about Jesus' being born, isn't it? " said Peggy.

" It's about the shepherds' coming to the stable to see the baby Jesus," said Peter.

" Yes, it's about all that," said Mother. " But it is *more!* It is being happy and giving thanks that the baby who was born was not just another child coming into the world, important as that is. It is celebrating the coming of God's own Son, who shows us and tells us that God's love is the greatest gift of our whole life."

" That's too hard to understand," said Peter. " I wish I could have been out in the field when those shepherds got scared by the angels' singing! "

" I wish I knew why Jesus had to be born in a stable," said Peggy.

" That's why we all need to take some time to get *ready* for Christmas," said Mother. " We need to try to under-

stand better what we are celebrating. Let's play a game. It's called ' I Wish . . .' about Christmas — with wishes that would help us to be truly ready."

" O.K.," said Peter. " I wish that I could have stood out in the field and heard the singing about ' Glory in the highest.' I wonder what I would have felt like."

Peggy thought for a moment. " I wish that I could have

seen Mary holding the baby Jesus for the first time. I wish I knew what she was thinking about as she looked at him . . . about what he would be when he grew up, and what would happen to him."

Mother said, " I wish I knew how Mary and Joseph puzzled over why this child was born to them, and how they would bring him up to please God."

" Let's start reading little bits of the Christmas story every day, and then we can talk about it," said Peggy.

" Sure," said Peter. " We hear the whole thing so often we don't even listen anymore. Let's pretend we are the people who were there, and see how we would feel about everything."

" All right," said Mother. " We'll start right now with the bit in the beginning of chapter 2 in Luke, where it tells about Mary and Joseph's going to Bethlehem. Will you bring me the Bible, Peter. I'll read just a few verses to start with."

Have you ever felt as Peggy and Peter did? You might make some " wishes " of your own to help you get ready for celebrating Christmas. During the days that are left before Christmas Day, read Luke 2:1-20, a few verses at a time, and think about what they tell us of God's way of sending to his people his own best gift of love. Maybe you will feel like singing " Glory to God in the highest," too.

A PRAYER / *Thank you, God, that you love us so much that you sent your Son to show us your great love. We know that you have always been faithful in keeping your promises to your people. Thank you that Jesus trusted your love and was willing to live his life and go to death to prove that your plan can never be defeated by any evil. Thank you that Christmas is more than celebrating a baby's birthday. Thank you that it is celebrating your gift of love to us. Amen.*

Jesus Is a Special Person

DID YOU EVER WONDER HOW MANY DIFFERENT PEOPLE
knew that the baby Jesus was a very special person? There
was Elizabeth, Mary's cousin, who was overjoyed to learn
that the child was to be born. And of course there were
Mary and Joseph, who wondered about his coming and

waited anxiously for his birth. Then there were the shepherds, who learned the good news of Jesus' arrival while
they were out on the hills tending their flocks of sheep. " Let
us go over to Bethlehem and see this thing that has happened, which the Lord has made known to us." (Luke
2:15.) When they had hurried to the stable, and found
Mary and Joseph and the baby, they praised God for all that
they had seen and heard that night. They told everyone
what had happened to them. " All who heard it, wondered
at what the shepherds told them." (Luke 2:18.)

King Herod knew that there was something special about
this child. In fact, Herod was afraid that the newborn baby
might someday become the king and take away Herod's
throne.

Sometimes we forget that the three Wise Men, who told
Herod the news about Jesus, made their long journey to
find the young child not just because they were interested in
following a new star that had appeared in the sky. They
came to find Jesus because they too knew that he was to be
a king. The gifts they brought were truly " fit for a king."
The Wise Men knelt down before the child and gave joyful
thanks to God that they had found him. Then, in order not
to have to return to King Herod and tell him where Jesus
was, they went back to their homes by another route. This
part of the story is in your Bible in Matthew 2:1-12.

There are some other people who also knew that Jesus
was a very special person. We do not hear as much about
them at Christmastime as we do about Mary and Joseph, or
the shepherds and the Wise Men. One of these people was
an old man named Simeon. When Jesus was about six weeks
old, his parents took him to the Temple to give thanks to
God. This was the custom among the Jewish people, and
Mary and Joseph may have been much surprised when old
Simeon came over to them when they arrived quietly at the
Temple. The old man took Jesus in his arms and prayed:
" O God, I give thanks that I have seen this child who will

grow up and make known to all people your great love. Now I can come to the end of my life in peace and joy, because I have seen him as it was promised to me."

Another person about whom you may hear very little at Christmas is an old lady named Anna. Everyone who knew her thought she was very good and very wise. After Simeon had finished his prayer, Anna took the baby in her arms and she too prayed: " O God, thank you for this child who will grow up and teach people your goodness and love." Then Anna went back to her usual place in the Temple. She knew that Jesus was a very special child.

Christmas-
time

Ever since Jesus was born on that first Christmas, people everywhere have come to know that he is truly God's own Son. It is very important that you know this, too. It is because he is God's Son that he can make known to us, as no other person can, how great and powerful and loving God is. God wants you to know that Jesus is his gift of love to you at Christmastime. That's why Jesus is such a special person. And that's what Christmas is all about.

A PRAYER / *For your gift of love in Jesus Christ, we give thanks at Christmas, O God. May we accept your gift, and show our love to you by acting in love and thoughtfulness toward others. Forgive us when we forget that you love us. Help us to turn back to you again, and accept your love. Amen.*

Is Jesus a Real Person?

ALMOST EVERYONE HAS WONDERED ABOUT THIS QUESTION. Even grown-ups who have listened to sermons, read their Bibles, sung hymns, and talked a lot about Jesus still wonder sometimes, " Is Jesus really and truly real? "

No one we know today has ever seen Jesus walking down the street. No one can show us a photograph of him, or even

a picture drawn by someone who has seen him. No person can even say he has talked to Jesus in exactly the same way that person can talk to you and me. And yet, the church has always been made up of people who believe in Jesus and who are sure that he *is* real.

This is not easy to explain! In fact, no one can fully explain all about it. Because God is so great and loves his people so much, the gift he gave of his only Son is too great a gift to be completely understood by any human being. And yet, one of the most exciting parts of all this is that God gives us faith to believe in someone we cannot fully understand. As we accept this gift of faith, we find our believing growing and growing until we too can say we KNOW that Jesus is real . . . even when we cannot understand or explain all about it, either.

There are some things that help us to think about Jesus as a real person. We need to pay attention to them, and allow them to help us to know more about his life and the time when he lived on the earth. Look at a map of the world and try to find the countries now called Israel and Jordan. Look for them up where Asia and Africa are hooked together. In Jesus' time, this area was called Palestine. Here is where he grew up, living like hundreds of other Jewish boys. If you have a book that tells how people lived in long-ago Palestine, perhaps you can find a picture in it that shows the kind of house in which Jesus lived.

Look in your Bible to find Psalm 1 or Psalm 8. Here you can read some verses in your own language that Jesus probably read in Hebrew. If you have Jewish friends, perhaps they will take you to their synagogue, where you can see scrolls much like those from which Jesus read God's word in the synagogue of his time in Palestine.

> The sun shone bright in Palestine
> When Jesus went to play;
> The same bright sun shines down on boys
> In Israel today.

> The same bright moon and silver stars
> In Galilee tonight
> Were shining there when Jesus walked
> Beside the sea at night.

The same great God who sent his Son
To show his love and might
Still loves his people, hears our prayers,
And shows us what is right.

Read about the birthday of Jesus in Luke 2:1-20.

A PRAYER / *Thank you, God, that it is all right to wonder about Jesus. Thank you for grown-ups who know that
he is real; for ministers who can tell us about him; for the
Bible, which helps us to know him better; for all the ways
we learn about Jesus. Thank you for giving us minds to
think and wonder and believe with. Thank you for giving us
Jesus to tell us of your great love. Amen.*

Our Neighbors Celebrate

" MOTHER! CAN YOU AND DAD COME TO SCHOOL ON FRIDAY
night before our Christmas holiday begins? " asked Dick.
" We're having a special program. It's really great! "

" I think we can come," said Mother. " What's so great
about it? "

" Well," said Dick, " we're going to celebrate two holidays at one time. Some of us are going to tell about Christmas, and some of the kids are going to tell about Hanukkah
. . . that's a Jewish holiday. What is Hanukkah about, anyway? "

Mother looked a little puzzled. " I'm not exactly sure
what it's about. I know that it is sometimes called the Feast
of Lights. And I know that it comes around the time of
year when we celebrate Christmas. But I don't know *why*
there is a celebration called Hanukkah. I think I'll ask the
Goldens next door."

" O.K., Mother," said Dick. " I'm going to be one of the
shepherds in our part of the program. I have to have a

striped costume, Miss Brown said. I'm going skating with
Morris now. So long." And Dick was gone out the door.

That night at dinner, Mother said, " I told Mrs. Golden
that we wanted to know about Hanukkah. She gave me a
book that tells the story of why the Jewish people celebrate
it at this time of the year. After I finish the dishes, Daddy is
going to read it to all of us."

This is the story that Dick's father read:

Once long ago the Jewish people were under the rule of
a Syrian king named Antiochus, whom people called " the
madman." He had copied the ways of the Greeks and wanted
to make Greeks of everyone in his kingdom. He sent out a
letter ordering every nation to give up its own religion and
laws so that they might all be one people.

Among the Jews there were many who refused to pray to
any gods but the one true God. They kept their own laws
more strictly than ever before. They believed that if they
remained faithful to God, their nation would someday be
set free from this tyrant king. But the time seemed long in
coming. Many of the finest Jewish young men were put to
death because they refused to worship the king's gods. Finally, some of the men rebelled against the king and at-
tacked his soldiers. They broke down the Greek altars. Then
they had to flee to the hills and hide to escape the king's
anger.

Even from their hideout, however, they continued to make sudden swift attacks against the Syrian army. Finally they became so successful that the king sent out a whole army to fight them. The Jews learned of the Syrian plan for a surprise attack, and before the enemy could begin the battle, the Jews entered their camp and surprised them instead. It was a fierce fight, but the Jewish leaders had put such faith and courage into the little group of poorly armed men that they defeated the Syrians.

Now the Jews were free to go back to their city of Jerusalem. But what a sight greeted them when they arrived. The Temple was deserted and its gates were burned. The courts were grown up with weeds. A new altar had to be built. Some of the Jews worked at cleaning and repairing the Temple, while others stood guard. Finally the people were ready to gather in the Temple court to praise God and worship him according to their religious laws.

Then a terrible thing happened! The priests discovered that there was only one jar of pure oil left for the sacred lamp — the light that was never allowed to go out. There was enough oil to last only one day! Nevertheless, they poured the oil into the lamp and kindled the light. And a great wonder happened! The lamp burned for eight days and the light did not go out! By that time, new oil had been prepared, and the people were called to celebrate with gladness and thanksgiving.

The struggle was not over for the Jews. By and by, however, the Syrians were driven from the land and the Jews were free to keep the Sabbath, study their holy books, and keep the law of the Torah.

Today Jews light lamps at Hanukkah in remembrance of those long-ago days. They celebrate the courage of their leaders who fought so bravely for their right to worship God as they thought was right. They wonder at the lamp that burned for eight days with only one day's supply of oil. The holiday is a happy one, and there is joy and thanksgiving

that their people are still free to worship God and obey his
laws.

If you have neighbors who will be celebrating Hanukkah
at this season of the year, ask them to tell you more about
their holiday. Perhaps they will show you their special me-
norah, the eight-branched candlestick on which candles are
lighted to remind everyone of the eight days when the lamp
in the Temple remained burning long ago. You may learn
from them some of the Hanukkah songs and games that
help to make this an especially happy time of celebration.

A PRAYER / *Thank you, dear God, that many people
have had the courage to refuse to worship any other gods
than you. Help us to learn from our neighbors more of the
story of your faithfulness to your people ever since men
have told about it. Help us to understand that they are celebrating your love and faithfulness, too. Amen.*

The Teachings of Jesus

IV

I F YOU KNOW WHAT YOUR CHILDREN ARE
thinking about Jesus and his teachings, you are fortu-
nate parents indeed! Boys and girls have many questions
that can become either stumbling blocks or doors that lead
them into further questioning. It is your job to try to sort
out some of the questions that can be answered with factual
information, some that can be answered only by the children
themselves, and some that need to be searched out together.
For the teachings of Jesus have a way of escaping us when
we are looking for " pat " answers about " right " and
" wrong." His words are more apt to lead us deeper into
questioning and wondering than they are to give us easy
answers. His life shows us how impossible it is to set boundaries and draw lines if one is to live a life of love as Jesus
did.

We believe that God has revealed himself in all his full-
ness in Jesus Christ. We want to share with our children the
stories about him that are part and parcel of our Christian
heritage. We want these stories to help our children know
God, and to grow in their response to him so that their lives
will truly be made new.

It is difficult to share with our children this kind of understanding if our own lives have remained untouched by
Jesus and his words. If love and forgiveness are still only
words, then it will be difficult to speak of them as more
than words to our children. On the other hand, if God's
mercy and grace are recognized as active forces in our lives,
we find it natural to talk about Jesus' *way* instead of his
words.

The following sections, while they are based primarily on
the teachings of Jesus, do not set forth any hard-and-fast
rules of behavior or standards of conduct. It is our hope
that children will come to understand something of Jesus'
teachings about love, forgiveness, mercy, and prayer. Then,
in the light of their understanding, they will make their own
decisions about whether or not to follow in his way. They

will choose for themselves whether or not they will run the risks of loving and forgiving those who may return only hatred and ridicule. Or harder yet, they must choose whether or not to pay attention to Jesus and his teachings in a world that seems to get along very well without them!

Two Mistakes

RANDY KING'S FATHER AND MOTHER WERE AWAKENED ONE night by the B'rrring-B'rrring of the telephone. It was Randy's uncle, calling to say that Grandmother King was very sick, and would they please come the very next day to see her. It was very important that they wait not even one day.

The next morning Mother said in her most serious-sounding voice, " Randy, I am going to ask you to do a very grown-up thing. Daddy and I must go at once to see Grandmother. We cannot get home until about eight thirty this evening. Do you think that you could come home from school, feed Rover, bring in the milk from the back porch, and take care of the house until we get back? Mrs. Porter is away visiting her daughter, and I do not have time to try to find someone else to come and stay with you. I will leave some cold chicken and potato chips for your supper, and you can get some ice cream from the freezer."

Randy jumped up from his chair, and stood straight and tall. " Sure, Mom! I'm old enough to take care of things. Don't you worry. I have my key and I'll come right home and I'll . . ."

" All right, dear," said Mother. " But don't forget the milk. And remember that Rover chews shoes, so don't let him go upstairs! Go along, now. The school bus is due in four minutes. Good-by, and have a good day! "

That afternoon Randy jumped out of the school bus and ran up the driveway. It was great to be left in charge of things! He unlocked the door, dropped the key on the table in the hall, and started for the kitchen. Rover whined and barked, and jumped up to lick Randy's face the minute he saw him. Quickly Randy emptied Rover's food into his dish, and soon the little dog had eaten every bite! " Come on, Rover. Let's go for a run," said Randy.

Out the door and into the field they went. Randy saw the milk bottles as he raced by the back porch. " Oh, well, there's lots of time to take them inside later," he said to himself. " I'd rather play with Rover now."

After a while Randy was hungry. " Let's go," he shouted to his dog, and ran for the house. Inside he found the chicken in the refrigerator, along with some milk, and potato chips in the big can. As he emptied the milk into his glass, he thought about the bottles on the porch. I'll get them when I finish eating, he thought. There's plenty of time.

Just then Randy saw the television guide lying on top of a pile of papers that Mother had stacked on a kitchen chair. " Let's see . . . today is Tuesday . . . it's nearly six thirty . . . hey! " Randy found that a great-sounding war movie was about to begin! He never watched television at this time of day because the family was always eating supper. And besides, he had agreed to look at only a few special programs on school days. But no one would know this time! The show would be over before his parents got home . . . and maybe he could do his homework during the commercials!

Randy ran upstairs to the little room where the television set was and turned it on. He curled up in the big armchair. Just as the movie was beginning, he heard Rover's pat-pat-pat out in the hall. " Go downstairs, boy," he called. " That's a good dog. Go on."

What a movie it was! Guns and tanks and lots of noise! Then, right in the middle of the biggest battle, Randy heard car wheels scrunching on the driveway. He ran to the top of the stairs just in time to see his mother opening the front door. Rover raced out of the bedroom proudly carrying in his mouth one of Daddy's new black shoes, well chewed and scratched.

The guns in the television movie were making such a racket that Randy scarcely could hear Mother say, " Hello, dear. We're home early. Daddy thought we should not stop

to eat along the way so that we would not have to leave you alone so long. How did things go? "

Let's stop the story right there! You can finish it for your-self if you want to! It doesn't have any *real* ending anyway. The story is trying to tell you about two mistakes that Randy made.

First, Randy decided that he could do what he liked while his parents were away. Second, he thought he would have plenty of time to do what he was supposed to do before they returned. Randy did not intend to get into trouble! But he had to face the consequences of his two mistakes.

You may be surprised to know that Jesus once told a para-ble to remind people of these same two mistakes. Read in your Bible in Luke 12:41-46 about a servant whose master went away and left him to take care of the household. The verses tell what the master will do if the servant acts as Randy did in our story.

One reason that Jesus told this story was to remind us that we cannot think about God and obey him only at those times when we want to remember him. We cannot pretend some-times that God is not present, and decide to do exactly what we please. Jesus was also trying to tell us that it is wrong to act as though we have plenty of time to think about God *later* — after we do all the things we want to do first! God is always present, and we cannot shut him away when we want to, or pretend that he does not know what we are do-ing and saying. Just as he always loves us and forgives us when we ask him, he expects us to remember him and try to live as he intends his people to do. When we make the mis-takes about God that Randy made, we have to face the con-sequences, too.

A PRAYER / *Dear God, help us not to forget about you when we want to have our own way instead of your way for us. Help us to learn to love you better. Thank you for al-*

ways loving us and forgiving us when we make mistakes. Amen.

A Preacher Who Was Afraid

ONCE LONG AGO THERE LIVED A YOUNG MINISTER NAMED Timothy. His church was very young, too, and Timothy worked very hard trying to help his people understand what God expects of those who believe in Jesus and accept him as their Lord. Many of the people were older than Timothy, however, and some of them thought that they were also much wiser than their young minister. Sometimes the congregation listened and agreed with Timothy. At other times they would *not* listen and they would *not* believe him.

All of this made young Timothy feel very discouraged. He was lonely, too, because his best friend — and the one person who could tell him what to do — was far, far away. One day, as Timothy was wondering what might happen to him if he kept on preaching and teaching about Jesus in ways that his people refused to believe, a messenger brought him a letter. In those long-ago days, letters were very special! Timothy knew that someone must have something very important to tell him. What could it be? Who could have written this letter? He turned it over, broke open the seal, and began to read.

" Timothy, my son . . ." was the way the letter started. Timothy could hardly believe his eyes! This must be from his good friend, the one man who could give him the advice he needed so desperately.

The young minister read on. " Do not let the people in your congregation look down on you just because you are younger than they are. Remember all that your grandmother and your mother have taught you about believing in Jesus, and about trusting his love and forgiveness always. Try to remember, also, what you have heard me tell about Jesus

Christ. As you go about your work of teaching and preaching, do not be afraid of the hardships that may come to you.
You must never fear what others will do to you because of
your own strong faith in Jesus. Go on preaching the good
news of God's love, and do the work he wants you to do.
God's love be with you."

If you want to know more about what was in Timothy's
letter, look in your Bible for the books called I and II Timothy. The young minister's friend gave him good advice
about standing up for what he believed was right, and told
Timothy not to be afraid to speak the truth at all times.
Read the words of II Timothy 1:7-8 and think how Timothy
must have felt as he read them long ago. Do you think that
they would have given you courage if you had been in Timothy's place?

Even today, long after the letters were read by the young
minister who was afraid, these words have much to say to
anyone who is trying to live as a faithful follower of Jesus.
It is never easy to go against the crowd, or to keep on doing
and saying what you believe is right and true, when people
are making fun of you or threatening to do you harm. Here
is some especially good advice for you to remember: " For
God has not given us a spirit of fear, but a spirit of power
and love and a sound mind. So never be ashamed of bearing
witness to our Lord " (II Timothy 1:7-8).

A PRAYER / *Dear God, who gave strength and courage to those who in times past followed Jesus, help us today to remember how people trusted in you for help when they were afraid. Help us to trust you when it is hard to follow your way of love as Jesus teaches us. Thank you for the special joy that comes when we know that we have been faithful and have stood up for what we believe about you. Amen.*

Road Signs

DO YOU REMEMBER THE LAST TIME YOUR FAMILY TOOK A trip over strange roads that none of you had ever traveled before? What did someone do before you started out? Chances are he asked for directions from a person who had been there before, or who knew the way. Perhaps he went to the gasoline station or the office of the automobile club and asked for a road map.

On the other hand, maybe someone has asked you for directions to one place or other. Was it to a faraway city? Or was it the way to a store, your school, or your church?

Think about some of the directions you have given or received. Sometimes they tell you to get on a big expressway and travel for a long way until you come to a certain exit,

where you are to turn off onto another highway or onto a side road. These are easy directions to follow, since once you are on the right road, you do not have to worry about turns or crossroads or where to go next. You just stay on the road until you come to the exit marked with the number where you are to get off.

Sometimes the directions are not that easy to follow. You may have to count a specific number of blocks, or pass so many traffic lights, or go a certain number of miles. Perhaps you must look for a crossroad with a particular name, or some building or landmark that designates the place where the directions tell you to turn.

You may choose to follow a road map that has the route marked on it with a wide line that goes east and west, north and south, or wherever the right road is. Then someone must watch the map carefully so that you stay on the route.

No matter what kind of directions you are following, one thing is sure. If the person directing you knows the right way to the place where you want to go, and if his directions are good ones, you will get to your destination if you do as he says. If you do not follow the directions, you may end up in the wrong town or waste time wandering around on the wrong roads. You may even miss the event you were going to see if there was a certain time you had planned to arrive.

When God created the world and the people to live in it, he did not say, " Now that's that! I'm finished with my part of the job. Let the people get along the best way they can." No, God has a plan for his world. He intends that every person shall be free to decide for himself how to think and act. But God also intends that all people shall learn to live together in love and kindness so that the world will be a happy one. Therefore, God did not make a long list of rules that everyone would be forced to follow. However, God does give very careful directions that point the way to the kind of life he wants for his people.

God's directions are a lot like the road signs you look for

on a trip. He does not tell us that we *must* go his way, but he does say that if we go one way, we will arrive at certain results. If we choose another direction, we will find a different situation. God is directing us toward the kind of useful and worthwhile life he wants us to have. Therefore, his road signs point that way and no other. We are free to make wrong turns, change our minds about where we are going, or try out other routes on our own. But God never changes the destination that he wants us to reach, and his directions are never wrong ones. His landmarks are never torn down or replaced. His way is always sure.

We could save ourselves a great deal of trouble if we would decide to go where God wants us to go, and be what he wants us to be. We can learn the directions he gives us through the teachings of the Bible and in the life of Jesus. Others around us who are trying to follow his way are often our guides, also. We can trust God and do our best to follow his directions, knowing that he is always ready to help us get back on the right road when we make mistakes.

You might like to read Psalm 119:105 and remember the words as you think about the part of your road you must travel today.

A PRAYER / *Dear God, thank you for giving us directions for traveling on the roads that are our everyday life. Help us to pay attention to them, to read them carefully, and to follow them the best way we can. Forgive us when we make mistakes, and when we decide that our own way is better than yours. Thank you for loving us so much that you are always ready to help us to get back on the right road. Amen.*

Gods for Sale

HAVE YOU EVER HAD A GOOD-LUCK CHARM THAT YOU WORE to bring you luck when you were going to play in a baseball game or take a big test? Have you ever gone to a museum where there were statues of gods worshiped by people whose religion is different from yours?

For as long as anyone can remember, men have always liked to have figures or objects of the gods they worshiped. It seems that a person can be more sure that the god really is there, listening to him when he prays, if the god can be seen and touched.

Long ago, when God was teaching his people that he is the one true God, and that there were no other gods before him, he knew that they would want to make statues and idols, too. One of the commands God gave to Moses begins, " You shall not make for yourself a graven image, or any likeness of anything that is in the heaven above or the earth beneath, or that is in the water under the earth; you shall not bow down to them or serve them " (Exodus 20:4). You can read these words in your own Bible, for God does not want *you* to worship anyone but himself. God does not want any of his people to depend on good-luck charms or figures that are made by man. God wants people to know him by the way he loves and cares for them, not because they have a statue that is supposed to look like him.

Once the apostle Paul got into trouble in the city called Ephesus over this very thing. The people there worshiped the goddess Diana. On almost every street corner you could buy a silver figure of Diana, for everyone wanted to please her in order to have good luck in business and to keep from having all kinds of trouble. The men who made these statues worked especially hard to have a big supply on hand for the festival time when people came from all around to worship at the temple of the goddess Diana.

" Great is Diana of the Ephesians! " they would shout.
" Come buy a statue of the goddess."

Festival time usually brought more business to the sellers
of the statues than any other time in the year. It was then
that Paul arrived in Ephesus. Listen to what he said to the
people:

" Gods that are made by men's hands are not gods at all!
You are wasting your money buying these statues. They
have no power. It is wrong to worship such gods. I have
come to tell you of the one true God who loves you, and
wants you to worship only him. You are to believe in him
and love him. There are no gods to buy for those who put
their trust in the true God. You are asked to obey him! "

Many of those who heard Paul believed what he was saying. They wanted to trust in the one true God who loved
them and cared about them. They wanted to become followers of Jesus. They stopped buying the statues of Diana!

The men who made the little figures of the goddess were frightened. " Our business is being ruined," they said. " We would have been sold out by now if that Paul had not come preaching all those lies about there being only one true God — who doesn't want people to buy our statues! Look, here are the trays still full of our best statues! If we let that madman Paul get away with this, the next thing we know, he will destroy the temple itself. He is an enemy of our religion! We must get rid of him."

Finally the people became so stirred up by all this talk that they started out to find Paul. " Get rid of him! Save our goddess! Save our business! " shouted the leader of the silversmiths.

No one knows what might have happened to Paul if his friends had not learned in time that the mob was coming to get him.They kept him away from the crowds until the city rulers were able to bring order again. When everything was quiet, Paul gathered his friends around him to say good-by. He knew that it was time to go on to preach in other places about God's great love.

God understands that his people want to be *sure* that he loves us and hears our prayers. He knows that sometimes it would be easier to have a statue to talk to or to touch, or to make promises to, or to blame when things go wrong. But God keeps telling us that he is not that kind of God! If we will listen and learn, and trust him, then we will understand better that he is so great and loving and powerful that no man could ever make a statue to take his place.

You can read the story about Paul and his troubles with the silversmiths in Ephesus in your Bible in Acts, chapters 19 and 20.

A PRAYER / *Thank you, O God, that no one can make a statue that looks like you. Teach us to learn what you are like by listening to the words of Jesus and seeing how he lived your way of love as no one else has ever done. Help us to trust you even though we cannot touch you or see what you look like. Thank you that you are greater than anyone we can even imagine. Amen.*

Wheat Versus Weeds

HAVE YOU EVER PLANTED A GARDEN AND WATCHED THE new, young seedlings pop up through the warm, wet earth? Maybe you have sprinkled a few seeds in some dirt in a paper cup or a flowerpot to see what would grow. Have you ever watched your father or your brother working in the big fields planting crops that will grow and produce a good harvest?

Gardens and fields and little flowerpots are very much alike in one way when the seeds begin to grow. Can you guess what that is? There are WEEDS! If you have ever helped to weed a garden in the hot sun on a summer day, you must have wondered where the seeds all came from. Pull the weeds one day . . . and the next day there are more weeds right where the first ones were!

There is a parable in the Bible that sounds at first as though it contains advice about planting gardens and pulling weeds. You can read it in Matthew 13:24-30. It tells about a farmer whose workmen report to him that weeds are growing up among the wheat that he had planted in his field. " Was that not good seed you planted? " they ask him.

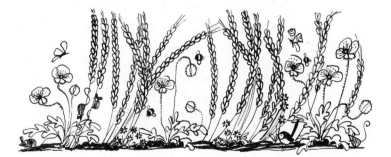

The farmer replies that there must have been an enemy who came and threw into his field the seeds that are growing up into weeds. When the workmen ask whether he wants them to get busy and pull out the weeds, the farmer gives them this answer.

" No," he says, " leave the field alone and let all the seeds grow together until it is time for the harvest. You might pull up some of the wheat if you try to pull out the weeds. Later on I will tell the reapers which to bundle up and carry off to be burned, and which to bring into the barns where I store my wheat."

At first it might sound as though the farmer did not care about raising a good crop. Let the weeds grow along with the wheat! But if you have weeded a *small* garden, you know how impossible it would be to even *try* to weed a big wheat field! The farmer knew that only at harvesttime would he be able to separate the good wheat from the weeds. " Let them grow together. The time for sorting out will come later."

This parable, like many others that Jesus told, is not really about farming at all, even though it talks about wheat and weeds. Jesus was trying to help people understand that in God's Kingdom, only God can judge who is good and who is bad. Only God knows when a person is growing to be like a weed or like a good stalk of wheat. And if a farmer is wise enough to know that he cannot weed his wheat field, think how much more unwilling God is to allow anyone to go around trying to get rid of the " bad " people in his world. God knows that the " good " and the " bad " must go on living together in his world until *he* knows when it is the right time to separate one from the other.

Parables are puzzling because they never tell us all the answers to the questions they make us ask. That is one reason why Jesus told them. He wanted people to wonder and think and grow in their understanding of how God's Kingdom is different from anything man might think up. God's ways of dealing with his people in love and forgiveness are different from all other ways of treating people. He is willing to take more risks on us than we would take on someone else.

Sometimes, after you puzzle and think, and still cannot find answers to all your questions, you have to remember that God does many things in his own way just because he is God. Therefore, he is the only one who understands fully all his reasons for doing things the way he does.

What questions do you think the people asked Jesus after he told them this parable? What would you have asked if you had been there? Read the verses again and think about the weeds and the seeds as people, the wheat field as God's world, and the farmer as God. Does it seem any easier now to understand?

A PRAYER / *Thank you, God, for taking care of us, no matter whether we act like " weeds " or like " good wheat." Help us to grow and become the persons you want us to be. Forgive us when we waste the time, health, and ability you have given to us — when we act like " weeds." Amen.*

Are You Poor?

" POOR JANEY! " " POOR OLD MAN! " " POOR MOTHER! " How often have you heard people speak of a person by referring to him as " poor " somebody or other? What does it mean to be poor?

Have you ever been so hungry that you thought you might never again have enough to eat? Not just hungry for candy bars, or some lunch or dinner when it was late — but really and truly hungry without knowing when you would have something to eat ever again?

Most people in our country have seldom been this hungry. To be sure, many people need *more* to eat, or to wear, or a better place to live. But few are so poor that they cannot find help somewhere. We are learning to take better care of those whom we call " poor " because they are in need.

There is another way in which many of us are " poor " without knowing it. Jesus tried to tell people this, but often-times they did not understand what he was saying. How can anyone have plenty to eat, clothes to wear, a nice house — and still be called " poor "?

Jesus said that people who thought only about themselves, and who tried to shut others out of their lives, could be called " poor." Someone has said that we are poor because we do not " belong to one another." What do you think that means? If God created man in his own likeness, making him the most precious of all that he created, then one person must also be precious to another person. Each of us must have worth and value to every other man. Jesus tried to tell us that if we go on living as though we were the only impor-tant persons in the world, as though what happens to us is all that matters, if we can forget all about the needs of oth-ers — then we are " poor " in the worst possible way.

Jesus gave his life so that every person, no matter how little money or skill or importance he has, might know God's love for him. If we do not treat people whom we meet and know as important and valuable human beings, then we are " poor " people living in the midst of the wealth of people God has made.

Think about your own friends. What would your life be like if you had no friends? Are you a good friend only when it is not too much bother, or are you a true friend? Do you try to make new friends among boys and girls, or grown-ups, when you are the one who has to speak first or smile first? Do you care enough about the people who have few friends to try to be friendly to them at least once in a while? Do you treat your friends as you want them to treat you?

There is a familiar story in Luke 10:29-37 about a man

who was a real friend to an injured traveler whom he found lying along the road. You probably call it the story of the good Samaritan. Read it again, and think about what Jesus was teaching us by telling such an incident. People who act like the good Samaritan will never be " poor " in wealth that is measured in God's people.

A PRAYER /   *Dear God, help us to remember those who have no home or not enough food to eat or clothing to wear. Help us to look for ways to share what we have with others. Teach us not to be " poor " for lack of friends, or because we do not want to be bothered with other people. Teach us how to show our love for you by showing love toward others of your people who are all precious in your sight. Help us to remember that " the Lord God made us all." Amen.*

Over and Over Again

IF ONE STORY IS TOLD OVER AND OVER AGAIN IN THE SAME book, it must be an important story, especially if the book is as important a book as the Bible. Although the words are not exactly the same, one story is found in three different places in your Bible. Here is where you can read it and see for yourself what the story is about: Mark 2:23-28; Matthew 12:1-8; Luke 6:1-5. See if you can decide what the story tells that is so important.

In the land where Jesus lived, there were great fields of grain that provided food for both the people and their animals. One day Jesus and some of his friends were walking through such a grainfield. Some of the men were hungry, so they picked some of the grain and ate it. Probably no one would ever have said a word about this except for one thing — it was the Sabbath Day! There was a rule in the book of Jewish law saying that it is wrong to work on the Sabbath. And picking grain was work! Even when a person picked just enough grain to eat in order to keep from being hungry, that was work!

The Pharisees wasted no time in accusing Jesus of allowing his friends to be lawbreakers. "Look what they did," said the Pharisees. "Certainly you must know that it is against the law to pick grain on the Sabbath. That is work, and work is forbidden on this day."

Perhaps Jesus shook his head a little sadly as he asked them, "Have you not read what our great King David did when he and his companions were hungry? Don't you remember how he went into the house of God and took some of the bread that was meant for no one but the priests to eat? King David took the bread and gave it to some of his friends so that they could eat and would not be hungry. It is better to show God's love to others than to worry over breaking a rule about working on a certain day of the week."

The Pharisees did not like what Jesus was saying one bit! They did not like to be reminded that their great hero, King David, had really broken the rule about eating the priests' bread in the Temple. But Jesus told them over and over again, in many stories and by many parables, that the most important rule of all is to love God and show that love by acting in kindly and thoughtful ways toward all men.

It is easy to shake our heads at those Pharisees of long ago, and to think that they certainly should have caught on better to what Jesus was trying to tell them. Why couldn't they see that it is better to keep one commandment about loving God and your neighbor instead of worrying about keeping the many, many rules about every little thing? But you and I sometimes act as though we have not " caught on " to Jesus' teachings. We make all kinds of excuses for not showing love to our neighbors, and even our friends, not to mention our enemies! We like to feel that we are doing a pretty good job of it if we keep the " rules " about kindness and thoughtfulness whenever it is *easy* to do this. But Jesus will not let us be satisfied with this kind of obedience any more than he would let the Pharisees feel satisfied about obeying the countless rules that were in their law.

Jesus insists that we too must love God with all our hearts, minds, and strength, and our neighbors as ourselves. Read these words in Matthew 22:36-39. Maybe you can say the commands over to yourself today as you try to live in the way they teach us. It is easier to say the words than to put them into action! But God promises to give strength to anyone who truly wants to make these the two most important rules of his life.

Read together Matthew 12:1-8.

A PRAYER / *Thank you, dear God, for teaching us your way of love. Help us to understand Jesus' teachings about not worrying over keeping a lot of little rules, but learning to love you and our neighbors instead. Thank you for forgiving us when we do not show love. Help us to try always to keep the important rules about loving you. Amen.*

God's Forgiving Love

" DOES GOD STILL LOVE ME EVEN WHEN I DO WHAT I KNOW is wrong? " Have you ever wondered about that? Have you ever wondered whether God loves people more when they are being good than when they are doing wrong?

There is a puzzling story in the New Testament about this question. You can read it in your Bible in Luke 15:11-32. After you think about it for a while, you may begin to find in it some ideas that will help you to answer the question for yourself. Perhaps the words used by the writer of the Bible story are strange to you. The following way of telling it may help you to understand it better.

Jesus told the story one time when the Jewish leaders were complaining because he was being friendly with those people whom the leaders called " sinners." Jesus told about a man who had two sons, the younger of whom asked his father for the share of the property that would one day be his. He wanted it right away instead of having to wait for it. The father agreed, and the young son took his wealth and went off to a faraway country. There he spent all that he had foolishly, wastefully, and selfishly. Finally he had no money with which to buy even a little food, so he went to work in the fields feeding pigs. He was so hungry that he would gladly have stuffed himself with the food the pigs were eating, but no one would give him anything at all.

Then he came to his senses and decided that he would go back home where even his father's hired helpers had more food than they could eat. There was no use in staying away and starving when there was plenty to eat at home.

The young son started back. His father, who had been sorrowing over his son's absence, learned of his coming and sent his servants to prepare a good dinner. Everyone was to gather to rejoice over the return of the son who had stayed away from his father and his home for such a long time.

As soon as the young son saw his father coming out to meet him, he began to beg his forgiveness for all the wrong that he had done. " I don't deserve even to have you call me your son," he said.

But the father did not beat him or scold him, or tell him to go back to the people on whom he had spent all his money. Instead, he put his arms around his son, kissed him, gave him clean clothes, and led him into the house for the feast.

The other brother soon discovered what was going on when he came in from working in his father's fields. He was furiously angry! " Look how I have worked for you all these years while my brother was off having a good time spending all the money you gave to him! You never had a big celebration like this for me. Now look what a fuss you are making over my brother's return."

The father replied, " But, my dear son, you have been here with me all the time. You know that everything I have is yours. But now we must celebrate over the return of your brother, because we thought he was lost from us. I thought that he was dead, but now he is alive and has come home to us. We must all rejoice! "

The story ends right there. What do you suppose the older brother did? How would you have felt if you had been in his place? Was the father being fair?

After you have puzzled over these questions, think how you might have felt if you had been the son who returned and was so warmly welcomed — especially after all the terrible things that had happened to you. Does this tell you anything about the greatness of God's love? or about the greatness of his love for people who get " lost " from him when their own selfish or foolish acts take them away from his loving care? It *is* puzzling, isn't it? But it's well worth thinking about.

Read the story in Luke 15:11-32.

A PRAYER / *Dear God, sometimes we are puzzled over your kind of love. Thank you that your love is not just like the way we love our friends and families. Thank you that it is so big we can never quite understand how big it really is. Thank you that you love us when we need love the most — even when we do wrong or foolish things. Help us always to want to come back to your loving care, and to remember that you want us to come back even more than we want to come. Amen.*

Do This! Don't Do That!

DO YOU EVER GET TIRED OF GROWN-UPS' TELLING YOU what to do? or how to do it? Do you ever wish that there were no rules that you had to follow and no laws that you had to obey? Do you wish that you could do just what you wanted to do all the time?

Would you be surprised to know that Jesus got into trouble with the people of his time over the matter of obeying rules? When Jesus lived in Palestine, there were laws for almost everything anyone had to do. There were laws about washing your hands and laws about the kind of clothing you should wear. There were laws about what you could and could not do on the day called the Sabbath. Because these were all written down in special books, people could not laugh at them or decide to pay no attention to them and do as they pleased. The laws were important, and anyone who wanted to be counted as obedient to God tried to follow

them very carefully.

How did Jesus get into trouble over these laws? If you will read in your Bible the verses in Luke 18:10-14, you will find there a story about two men who went to the Temple to pray. One man, a Pharisee who paid careful attention to keeping all the laws, thanked God that he was not like other men. He spent a long time telling God how much money he gave to the Temple, and about how he kept all the rules and laws all the time. He especially pointed out to God a tax collector who had also come to the Temple to pray. The Pharisee gave thanks to God that he was not like that tax collector who did not keep all the laws.

Then the tax collector began to pray. " I am sorry for the many wrong things I have done," he said, speaking in a low voice so that none of the people around would notice him and try to hear what he was saying. He did not say anything about how well he had kept the laws. He did not make excuses for breaking some of them. He only asked God to forgive him for his wrongdoing.

When Jesus told this story, many of the people expected him to point out the good Pharisee and praise him for having kept the laws. Instead, Jesus said, " The Pharisee tried to set himself up as a real somebody in God's sight! But he was only boasting about how good he was."

The tax collector, however, did not pretend that he was better than he really was. He admitted his faults, and asked God to forgive him so that he would be strong enough not to keep on doing wrong. Jesus said, " The tax collector was the one who went away from the Temple having received God's mercy and forgiveness, not the Pharisee."

How do you think you might have felt if you had been listening to Jesus when he told this story? The people who heard him did not like what he said. Can you think of some reasons why?

Most of us like to tell about how good we are, and to have others praise us for our goodness. Jesus was trying to tell everyone that God's love is great enough so that we can admit our wrongdoing and still know that he loves and forgives us. When we know that we have done wrong, and admit that we would like to act differently, God is ready and able to help us to do what is right. God cares very much whether or not we want to obey him always. He is always ready to help us when we come to him honestly and sincerely.

Read together with your family Luke 18:10-14.

A PRAYER / *Dear God, sometimes we want you to think that we are a lot better than we really are. Sometimes we try to talk about other people when we should be admitting our own faults. Help us to be honest about our wrongs, and not to think that we are better than others because we keep rules that they may break. Teach us to follow your way of love as Jesus shows us and tells us of it. Amen.*

God's Ways—Or Man's Ways?

MANY TIMES IN THE LONG STORY ABOUT THE HEBREW people that we read in our Bible, God tells them, " My ways are not your ways." God is trying to make his people understand that his ways are far beyond any of the best ways or the greatest ways that any man can think of, no matter how hard a person tries. If this were not so, then some men might know as much as God — and God would not be God!

There are always many good and wonderful people to be found in every church, every town, and every place where men, women, and children gather. But no one of them can ever understand completely God's love and forgiveness. Think about yourself, and try to remember the last time someone did a mean thing to you or said something untrue about you. How long did it take before you stopped being angry with that person, and decided to show him that you had forgiven him? When you did forgive him, did you feel that maybe you would forgive him " just this once, but not if he did it again "? Or did you forgive him IF he would apologize or do something to show that he deserved your forgiveness? Sometimes we keep people *waiting* for our forgiveness so that we can " teach them a lesson " or keep them from thinking that they can push us around any way they please. In other words, we like the feeling of thinking that we can forgive or not forgive, just as we please.

God does not use his mercy and forgiveness in this way. His way is one of reaching out to man and wanting him to turn to God seeking forgiveness. God's way is to help man to *accept* forgiveness. It is man's way to make people *earn* forgiveness — to insist that someone must deserve it before he is forgiven. God's way is not an easy way for man to learn.

Sometimes it is very hard to understand God's way of

love, also. We often say that a person does not *deserve* God's love, because he acts in ways that make it seem as though he does not care at all about God's commands. We may say that to give love to such a person is not fair.

We often talk as though we have to earn God's love. This is not so. Jesus tried very hard to tell people this, but it was almost too much for them to believe that God could love his people so much that he practically throws love away on them!

The story in Luke 15:11-32 tells us about this kind of love. A young son takes his share of the money that his father planned to divide between his two sons. He spends it, and comes back home tired, hungry, and dirty, knowing that he has done wrong but hoping that his father will take him back even as a hired man. His father welcomes him warmly, but the older brother cannot understand why his father is making such preparations to show the young brother that he loves him and wants him home again. No one had ever given a big dinner for the stay-at-home brother!

The father tries to explain that he has been loving the older brother all the time. But now that the son who was far away is back, he has to find ways to show him that he still loves him, no matter what the son has done wrong. The young son *came home* to his father, and was welcomed with love. God loves those who are faithful to him and live in obedience to his way. God also loves those who turn back to him after having done wrong, asking for his love and forgiveness. God also loves those who refuse to return to him; he is sad over the troubles they make by their wrongdoing; he is always reaching out to call them to come home and accept his love.

This is God's way of love. It may not always seem " fair " to us, but then, it's God's way!

A PRAYER / *Dear God, whose love for us is so great that we cannot understand your way of love, teach us to trust you so that we will always turn back to you and ask forgiveness when we know that we have done wrong. Help us to choose wisely when we must make decisions about right and wrong. Thank you that we do not have to " pay for " our mistakes before we can receive your forgiving love. Help us to re- member your way of love when others hurt us and do wrong against us, and want our forgiveness. Amen.*

"I'll Pay Him Back!"

JIM BURST INTO THE HOUSE, BANGED THE DOOR BEHIND him, and threw his school bag into a chair. " I'll get even with him if it's the last thing I do," he muttered. " I'll think of a way to pay him back that he'll never forget, that's what I'll do! "

Mother looked up from the pie dough she was rolling out on the big board on the table. " Who made you look like a thundercloud? " she asked. " I'm glad I'm not the one you are going to do all that to! "

Jim grumbled some more. " It's that Barry Green. He thinks he's so smart! Today our committee was supposed to give our report on Indians and he told all the good stuff about the warriors and weapons and all that."

" How did that happen? " said Mother. " Didn't you all agree beforehand which part each of you would tell? "

" Sure we agreed! But Barry had to be first, like he always does, and he just kept on talking about our parts because he said it was the most interesting."

Mother shook her head. " I don't think Barry needs some- one to get even with him. I think he needs someone to help him."

Jim picked up his book bag and started upstairs. " He thinks he knows more than anybody! He doesn't want any help. He just wants everybody to stand back and let him be the big shot all the time! "

All week long Jim tried to think of a way to get even with Barry. He thought of dumping the contents of his desk onto the floor, but he knew Barry would find a way to get someone else to pick them up! He thought of telling Mr. Jenks, their teacher, about Barry, but he didn't know quite what to say without sounding like a tattler! What *could* he do?

When Mr. Jenks made the next project assignment, Jim found his chance. The committee of which he and Barry were part was to prepare a rock collection showing some of the steps in making arrowheads, some of the rocks used, as well as other minerals available in the part of the country where they lived. Jim quickly offered to bring a large sheet of cardboard on which to mount the rocks. He had it lying on a table, ready to be used, when the other boys got to school the next morning.

As usual, Barry took charge. " You were smart to find a table big enough to hold such a large piece of cardboard," he said to Jim. " We won't need to disturb it until I hold it up for the class to see. Let's fasten these rocks on good and tight so they won't fall off when we tip it up."

Jim chuckled, but said nothing. Every once in a while he whispered something to one of the other boys, but never to Barry. Jim could scarcely wait for the project to be finished!

On the day they were to give their report, Barry again claimed that he should show the rocks and speak first. This time no one argued with him. When Mr. Jenks called their group, Barry jumped up and hurried to the table. " We are going to show you the greatest rock collection you ever saw! " he said as he leaned over to pick up the display. Just as he started toward the front of the room carrying the collection, the cardboard bent right in the middle! The boys had managed to put all the heaviest rocks near the edges, and the weight was too much for the size of the cardboard. Rocks flew everywhere, rolling under the desks and along the floor! The display was in ruins.

Jim pretended to groan, but all the time he was watching Barry's face. Barry looked horrified and surprised and angry. Jim almost laughed right out loud, but remembered in time to keep on looking sad.

That night when he told his mother, she asked, " Do you feel better now about the other report? "

" What other report? " Jim asked, looking puzzled. " Oh, that one! I'd almost forgotten about it. I was too busy paying Barry back for it! "

" Then what good did this trick do? " asked Mother. " You boys have to do the project all over again, don't you? "

" Oh, Mother! You don't understand," said Jim. " I got even with Barry. I really paid him back! Don't you see? "

Almost everyone feels at one time or another as Jim did about Barry. Jim's mother asked a question that might make you stop to wonder whether Jim's way was the best way to act. What good did it do to " pay back " Barry? Can you think of other ways Jim might have acted?

If you will read Romans 12:17-21, you may find clues to what the followers of Jesus had to say about " getting even " and " paying back " for wrongs done to them. A good idea to remember is found in the words of verse 17, " Repay no man evil for evil."

A PRAYER / *Our Father, we admit that we often like to " get even " and " pay people back " when they have wronged us. Help us to try to find other ways of changing their actions toward us. Help us not to think we are being smarter than they are just because we think of tricks for " getting even." Thank you for your love that does not play tricks on us, but is always given freely to us when we come to you and are willing to accept your way. Amen.*

Someone Is Watching You!

WHO IS YOUR GREATEST HERO? IF YOU COULD CHOOSE ONE person for your ideal, and become exactly like him, whom would you choose? Are there people you imitate now in one way or another?

We all know friends or other people who are so kind or helpful or intelligent that we wish we could be like them. When one of these persons does something that we did not think he would ever do because the act is mean or wrong or dishonest, we feel disappointed. We say our hero has " let us down." Sometimes we find that we have been trying to imitate the wrong kind of person.

After you read the following story about two brothers, perhaps you will think about another idea regarding heroes and imitating other people.

Sammy and Paul were brothers. Sammy was only five years old, and Paul was his wonderful " big " brother — almost twelve years old! Sammy wanted to go everywhere that Paul went, and do everything just the way Paul did it.

Sometimes this made Paul angry. " Go away! Don't bother me! " he would say. " Little kids can't do what we can do. Go play with your own friends."

At other times it felt sort of good to have even your little brother think you were so great! Sometimes Paul bragged to Sammy about what he had done, even adding on just a little more than was true to make the story sound better. Paul was Sammy's hero, there was no question about that!

One day Father told Paul and Sammy that they could use his tools to build a wagon if they would promise to be very careful with them. "Please do not allow anyone else to use them if I am not here," said Father. "And be sure to put everything back in its place when you are finished."

The boys promised, and soon were at work out in the yard, trying to make the wheels stay on the wagon. Sammy watched and handed tools to Paul, who did most of the work, of course. Bert came over from next door to watch, and to say that he could probably make a better wagon!

Paul became cross at Bert's big talk and began to act as though he knew a great deal more about tools and wagons than he really did. He was showing off to Bert, and hurrying to finish the wagon so he could ride down the walk on it and make Bert jealous!

That night Father checked his tools and found that his new wrench was missing. He called Sammy and Paul and asked, "Where is my new wrench, boys? It is not in the place where I left it."

Sammy couldn't even remember what the wrench looked like! Paul remembered too well. He remembered that he had kept it in the wagon in case he had to tighten a bolt or something! It may have fallen out while he was riding . . . it might be lost forever.

Suddenly Paul had an idea. "That smart aleck Bert must have taken it," said Paul. "He was fooling around over here making fun of our wagon. I'll bet he picked it up and then dropped it somewhere instead of giving it back."

Father looked cross. "I asked you not to allow anyone else to use the tools, Paul," he said. "You were responsible for them."

Paul's explanation become more and more mixed up as he tried to put all the blame on Bert and not get into trouble himself. All this time Sammy listened and looked more and more puzzled. Every time he started to say something, Paul told him to keep quiet. Paul promised to look for the wrench, but he knew there was little chance of finding it!

Who was the " hero " who was being watched in this story? There is no famous or important person in it. Paul seems just like any boy who has a little brother like Sammy! Does Paul remind you of yourself? Did you ever stop to think that you might be a " hero " to someone else? What you do is always very important because you never know when " someone is watching you."

Read Ephesians 5:1-2. There you will find some advice about choosing the person to imitate yourself, so that you will be a good " hero " for others to imitate.

A PRAYER / *Dear God, help us to remember that there are others watching to see how we act and how we treat other people. Teach us to follow your way and imitate the kind of life that Jesus shows us how to live. Thank you that we need never be afraid of doing wrong when we imitate your way of love. Amen.*

That's Too Hard!

SUZY SAT IN CHURCH WITH HER PARENTS, LISTENING CARE-fully to what the minister was saying. This was a service of worship to which the children of the church had been especially invited, and Suzy had helped to give out the bulletins and tell people where to sit before she sat down beside her mother.

Now the minister was reading from the big Bible. " I will read some verses from Matthew, chapter 5, verses 43 to 45. Then we will think about them together."

(You might like to read these verses for yourself, so that you will know what Suzy was thinking about.)

Later, after the service, Suzy was walking home with her parents. " That was a helpful sermon our minister preached today," said Father. " He made me think about the way I treated that workman whom I caught cheating me last week. I was pretty hard on him, without being very helpful."

Suzy was quiet for a moment. Then she said, " I didn't like that sermon! What he said is too hard to do! How can you go around loving people who hate you? If you hated them the way they hate you, then they might stop! "

" Wait a minute," said Mother. " Who hates you, Suzy? What was the minister saying to *you* this morning? "

" It's like Father said . . . about the workman who cheated! " replied Suzy. " I'd make him go and get another job, that's what I'd do! "

" But that's your father's problem, not yours, Suzy," insisted Mother. " That's one reason why it's too hard for you. How do you think the minister meant that *you* could obey Jesus' teachings that he talked about this morning? "

" Have you made up with Sally yet in that fuss over who owes the fine on the library book you both were reading? " asked Father.

" Or have you done anything about David's bookcase where you turned the books upside down because you were angry at him? " asked Mother.

Suzy looked to see if her parents were teasing, but they both were very serious. " Well . . . no," said Suzy. " I told Sally if she didn't pay her share I would never speak to her again! She's not being fair not to pay. I don't like her anymore."

Father coughed and said, " H'mmmmm! I think I heard something in a sermon this morning that might help in that situation. I never would call you and Sally enemies . . . and yet you are not acting like friends! "

Suzy thought hard. " David's not my enemy, either. He's just a teasing big brother, that's what he is! But sometimes he makes me mad! "

Mother smiled and put her arm around Suzy as they walked along. " I know it's hard to follow Jesus' teachings

about showing love to those who make you cross, or who tease you too much. But it's not *too* hard if you remember that he wants you to start with things like that and learn how to be kind and loving as well as fair to your friends and family. Later on, when you may have some real enemies, you will have been learning what to do about them."

" That's right," said Father. " It's going to be hard for me to see if I can't help that workman we were talking about. But it won't be *too* hard, because God will help me. I'm glad it's not the first time I've tried to show love, though, or I guess I might feel just the way you do, Suzy! "

Have you ever decided that some of the teachings of Jesus were " too hard " for you? Think about them again. Someone has said that the longest hike always starts with the first step! Maybe you could choose one " first step " in trying to follow a hard teaching. If the teaching that Suzy heard from Matthew 5:43-45 is a hard one for you, as it is for most people, why not decide right now on one *first step* in following it — then do something about it. Be sure you ask God to help you, because he knows it is hard for you, too.

A PRAYER / *Dear God, help us not to try to hide behind the excuse that your way is "too hard" for us. Teach us to listen to the words of Jesus and try to follow them in the best ways we can. Help us and forgive us when we make mistakes, and help us to try again. Amen.*

Let Your Light Shine

"HONK! HONK!" WENT THE HORN ON AUNT BETH'S CAR as she pulled into the driveway at Karen's house.

Karen ran to the door and called, "I'll be there in a minute, Aunt Beth. I have to get my sweater."

Soon Karen and her aunt were driving along the road leading up into the mountains. Aunt Beth was teaching her class in high school about wild flowers, and she wanted to find a few specimens of rare plants to show to her students.

When they reached the lane that led into an old, abandoned farmyard, Aunt Beth parked the car. "Come along, Karen. We walk from here on. Up by that old pine grove is where I think I will find what I am looking for."

As they walked along, Aunt Beth kept stopping to look at this or that plant, to admire a butterfly, or to watch a bird swooping down on an insect. Finally they came to the pine grove, where Aunt Beth found the plant she wanted.

When they were in the car again and on the way home, Karen looked back at the mountain. "It's too bad so many lovely things go to waste way out there," she said.

"What is going to waste?" asked Aunt Beth.

"Oh, the wild flowers that nobody sees, the butterflies, and all the birds . . . everything we were looking at," said Karen.

"We saw it and enjoyed it, didn't we?" asked her aunt. "And I have a friend who comes here many times every summer, just to sit quietly and enjoy the beautiful things."

"Maybe other people come," said Karen. "It just seems

so deserted today."

Aunt Beth was quiet for a while. " Sometimes people are like that mountainside," she said. " We think we are not important, and that no one notices us. We never do anything very great. Yet we never *know* when someone is stopping to look at us or watch what we are doing."

" Miss Bond told us about a verse in the Bible that says we should let our light shine," said Karen. " Some of the kids laughed because they said it sounded as though you were supposed to keep your lights on all the time! "

" That's what I'm talking about," said Aunt Beth. " Jesus says we should let the sight of our actions toward others be like a light that may help other people know more about the way of love. Of course, we could be like clouds, too, and hide his way by our thoughtless and unkind actions. Whichever we do, someone is bound to see us and learn something from us."

" I don't ever think that anyone is looking at the way I treat people hoping to learn something from me," said Karen. " I only think about it when Mother or Daddy scolds me for being mean or unkind! "

" Learning to think about things like this is part of growing up," said Aunt Beth. " Let's stop here for an ice-cream cone! All this serious talk has made me hungry! How about you? "

Read Matthew 5:16 in your Bible. Sometimes we think that we should call attention to our good works and kind acts in order to have people tell us how good we are. Notice that the last part of this Bible verse says that the glory for our good deeds goes to God! We can let our light shine and know that men are looking at our good and kind acts, and yet not be proud, because we give the credit and glory to God, who helps us to live in his way of love.

A PRAYER / *Dear God, help us to remember that people look at us and our good and kind acts shining like a light. Help us not to act in unloving ways that will be like clouds to your way of love. Teach us not to be proud of our goodness, but to give the glory to you, for we know that we cannot follow your way of love without your help and guidance. Thank you for Jesus, who shows us how to act so that our lives will be like lights and not like clouds. Amen.*

Ingroup or Outgroup?

LONG AGO, BEFORE JESUS CAME TO SHOW ALL MEN THAT
God loves everyone, no matter what nation or race he belongs to, the Hebrew people tried very hard to live as God's
own nation. They worshiped him as the one true God. They
kept the laws that were written in their lawbooks. They gave
their money and their gifts to the Temple. They worked at
being obedient, God-fearing people.

But they kept making one mistake over and over. Because God had spoken to them, and made his promise to
them that he would always be with them to care for and protect them, they thought that God was only for *them*. They
were the ingroup, and they did their best to keep everyone
else " out." Around the outside of their Temple, in the place
where no one but the God-fearing Hebrews were allowed to
go, there was an inscription written so that all could read it.
The words warned everyone who was not a Hebrew that if
he came any farther into this Holy Place, he would very

probably be put to death. The holiest of the Holy Place was only for the ingroup.

When Jesus came, one of the hardest things for the Hebrews to believe was that God's love was for everyone, even for the people who did not obey all the Hebrew laws. They could not understand why the ingroup, who worked so hard to keep the law and to reject those who did not keep the law, should have to accept the outgroup so that all would be *one*.

One of the early Christian preachers tried to explain to some of his friends that those who had been kept far off were now made welcome through Jesus, who came to make all men one group. You can read his words in Ephesians 2:13-14.

Are you thinking that it was foolish of the Hebrews to feel this way about God, wanting to keep him for themselves and to shut others out? Are you saying that this is just something that happened a long time ago, but that now people know better? If so, I think you may be all wrong! People are still trying to keep themselves in their own groups, made up of people mostly like themselves.

How about your own friends? Do you choose them from boys and girls who are like you? Or do you have friends of different skin color, who come from homes different from yours, or who live in a part of town different from where you live?

Think about your church school class and ask yourself the same questions that you asked about choosing your friends. If your answers to all these questions show that your friends and classmates are all just like you, maybe you had better read Ephesians 2:13-14 again and remember that the words are for you, just as they were for the people who lived long ago.

It is easy to say that all men are one in Christ. It is not always easy to show that you really believe it! Are you part of the *ingroup,* or of the *one group* of God's people?

A PRAYER / *Dear God, who made all people to live as one, help us to choose our friends and acquaintances from all sorts of interesting boys and girls. Teach us to know and like many people, no matter what their race or color may be. Forgive us when we shut out others because they are different from us. Forgive us for trying to hold your love in our own ingroup. Thank you for sending Jesus to show us the joy of loving all your people. Amen.*

The Puppet Show

JANE AND MARTIN CLAPPED AND CLAPPED THEIR HANDS when the puppet show was over. They blinked when the lights went on, and they saw the tiny stage and the little puppet figures.

" How does he make them act so real? " asked Jane.

" I'd like to see how he works them," said Martin.

Uncle Max looked around for the man who owned the puppets. " I know him well," he said. " He's a friend of mine. I'll ask him to show the puppets to us if he has time before the next show."

Jane and Martin followed Uncle Max over to the stage. The owner greeted Uncle Max with a big smile and a big handshake. " These are my niece and nephew, Jane and Martin," said Uncle Max. " This is Paul the Puppet Man."

" Would you like to see the puppets and hold one in your hand? " asked Paul. " Come back here where I work them."

Martin saw the puppet who had been the fierce giant in the play. " Look! He's not much like a giant now," said Martin. " He's all saggy and crumpled up! "

" Hold these sticks and try to work the strings that make him stand up and move around," said Paul. " Don't get the strings twisted up."

Martin tried to make the giant look like the fierce giant, but the best he could do was to make his arms and legs jerk

around! " I'm no good at this," laughed Martin. " I can't make him do what I want."

Jane was trying to make the princess puppet dance gracefully up and down the stage, but she didn't have much more luck than Martin.

Paul the Puppet Man only laughed. " It looks easy, but it takes a great deal of practice to make a show run smoothly. I have worked at puppet shows for a long time, and now I can make my puppets do anything I want them to do — anything at all! "

Martin and Jane thanked the man for showing them the puppets, and started home with Uncle Max. Martin pretended he was the giant puppet and Jane danced along the sidewalk like the princess puppet.

" I'd like to be a puppet," said Martin. " Then I wouldn't have to think about watching the cars when I cross the streets, or studying my lessons for school, or washing my hands before lunch."

" I'd like to be a puppet, too," said Jane. " Then someone else could dress me, and tell me when to play and when to sleep, and I wouldn't have to worry about anything."

Uncle Max shook his head. " No, indeed! Not me. I would not like to be a puppet. But you two can be sort of puppets if you really want to," he said.

" How? " asked both Martin and Jane. " Tell us how! We'll try it."

" Think about the puppets. They do exactly what someone makes them do, without asking any questions or thinking about right and wrong. They never worry about how their actions will help or hurt someone else. It's every puppet for himself! Real people can be like that. I'm afraid I do a little of that myself," said Uncle Max. " But God didn't make his people to be puppets. He refuses to pull strings that make us do this or that. God gave us minds and hearts to think and feel with. He expects us to use them. And God is very unhappy when we act like puppets and let someone else pull the strings that tell us what to do."

" I guess I won't be a puppet after all," said Jane.

" Me either," said Martin. " It's harder to be a person, but I guess it's more fun! "

A PRAYER / *Dear God, sometimes it is easier to do what everyone else is doing, just like a puppet with someone pulling the strings, than it is to make up our own minds and take the consequences of our decisions and choices. Help us not to be like puppets, but to have the courage to live as you intend us to live, using our minds that you have given us. Thank you for not pulling strings and making us do certain things. Help us to make wise choices about what we do. Amen.*

"I Didn't See God!"

BRUCE CAME DOWN TO BREAKFAST ONE MORNING RUBBING his eyes and yawning. " I didn't want to wake up, because I was dreaming a great dream, Mother," he said. " I wanted to keep on dreaming it so I could see God! "

Mother looked puzzled. " Are you sure you are not still dreaming? " she asked. " How could you see God? "

Bruce started to drink his juice. " Well, this dream I had was about going up in a huge rocket — the biggest one in the world. It shot up higher than anything we can make now. I was riding in it, and I could make it go wherever I wanted. I decided that I would go up and up and up — higher than anyone. So I did! And when I got there, I saw a big sign. You know what it said? "

" Maybe it said, ' Bruce Peters, go home! ' " said Mother.

Bruce laughed. " Nope! It said HEAVEN! "

" You dreamed you were in heaven . . . according to your sign? " asked Mother.

" U'mmm h'mmmm," said Bruce with his mouth full of toast. " I looked all around, but I couldn't see God! That's why I wanted to stay asleep and keep on dreaming. Then maybe I'd get to him."

Mother sat down at the table and stirred her coffee. " Are you trying to tell me that you think our astronauts may some-day get to a place where they will find God waiting to greet them? " she asked.

" Well, we were talking about it at school," said Bruce. " One of the kids said that if heaven was up in the sky, then if someone went far enough, he ought to come to where God is! I guess I was thinking about that when I went to sleep . . . and that's why I dreamed about it. Will someone get to where God is, Mother? "

" No, Bruce. No matter how high or far out any man trav-els in space, he will never come to where God is. If man

could do that, then God would have to say, ' Well, now you
have caught up with me, and you know all about me, and
you are as great as I am! ' " said Mother.

" If we got as great as God, then he wouldn't be really
God, would he? " asked Bruce.

" You are quite right," said Mother. " God shows us in
many ways what he is like. Most of all, he has shown us by
sending Jesus to make known to us his greatness and power
and love. But God is greater and more powerful and more
loving than anyone can imagine, so there is never any limit
to God. There are no boundaries that man can put on him.
There are no lines we can draw to shut him in where we can
measure his love and power. And there is no one place
where God lives, the way we live here in this house. Because

God is God, and not a superman, he can be and is everywhere."

" I think an astronaut would be scared if he really thought he might run into God somewhere," said Bruce. " I don't think I really want to see God like that."

Mother opened the Bible that was on the bookshelf nearby. " Here is a verse I think you should remember, Bruce," she said. " It is in John 1:18. ' No one has even seen God; the only Son, . . . he has made him known.' "

Bruce thought for a minute. " Jesus is who makes God known, just as it says there, right? "

" Right," said Mother. " The next time you start wondering whether someone may run across God out in space, you remember this verse. Then start thinking about all that Jesus has made known to *you,* and you will be closer to seeing God than you ever will be in a rocket or a dream! "

A PRAYER / *Thank you, O God, that there is no danger that someone may find you out in space. Thank you that you are out there, and with us, and anywhere at all. Thank you that this is your world, and that you are not shut in the way man shuts things in with limits and boundaries. Thank you for always being greater and more loving than we can ever imagine you to be! Amen.*

Real Friends

JAMIE AND DAVE WERE FRIENDS — REAL FRIENDS! SOMEtimes they got angry with each other, but it never took long to straighten things out. " We can't waste time staying mad! " said Dave. " We have too many things we like to do together."

There was only one thing they *couldn't* do together. Jamie could not ride a bike. He tried once and fell off. He tried again and hurt his leg. He tried again — no luck! When peo-

ple began to laugh at him, he stopped trying. "Let's do something else," he said.

Year after year, when the other boys were riding bikes on the first warm spring days, Jamie would look at the bikes on his front porch. He would kick at the tires and turn the handlebars. Sometimes he would try to ride, when no one was watching. But he just could not ride a bike!

Then one spring Jamie decided that he would ride a bike

if it was the last thing he ever did! His big brother saw the look on Jamie's face that meant " I will! "

" I'll help you, Jamie," he said, and went along beside the bike to steady it. At first it seemed as though the same thing that had happened every other year would happen again. Jamie fell off once . . . twice . . . three times. But each time he got back on the bike and tried again. Just when his brother and all his friends thought for sure that he would give up, Jamie rode for half a block without falling off! His brother shouted and jumped up in the air.

" Try it again! " said Jamie's brother, and Jamie did. This time he rode a whole block! Then he rode farther and farther, until he was riding and not falling off even once! It was a wobbly trip, and he did not go very fast, but he was riding.

While this was going on, Dave was riding his own new bike up and down the back alley. " I'll stay away so he won't think I'm watching," said Dave. " It feels funny to have people watching you make mistakes."

When Dave saw Jamie going around the block for the second time, he started after him on his own bike. It was a sleek, fast, well-balanced bike, and Jamie looked at it — then down at his own smaller, clumsy one. Dave looked too. Suddenly he said, " Here, Jamie. Try my bike. I'll bet it's even easier to ride."

The boys traded bikes, and Jamie started off. Faster and faster he rode. He could hardly believe his own eyes! A little while ago he couldn't ride at all. Now he was riding as fast as Dave! Up the slope and across the grass he went. Back down the street and around the corner. All the time with Dave trying to keep up on the clumsy old bike of Jamie's.

The next day after school both boys hurried home to get their bikes. Once again Jamie was on Dave's bike and Dave rode Jamie's. Both boys looked so happy that people smiled at them as they raced by.

That night, as David was going to bed, he said to his

father, " Did you see Jamie riding a bike today? It was really great! He can ride as well as anybody now. He feels so good he can hardly stand it! "

" I thought it was your bike he was riding," said Father. " Your new bike that you wouldn't lend anyone! "

Dave grinned and looked down at his shoes. " Yeah! It *was* my bike. But you know, Dad, when he finally found that he could ride, I just wanted him to have the fun of a real ride! That old bike of his was too little and too heavy to go very fast! You have to work like crazy to make it go at all. So I thought how he would feel flying along on mine . . . and I just wanted him to have that feeling! He deserved something special, he worked so hard to learn to ride."

When Jesus talked to his disciples about showing love toward one's friends, he told them, " Greater love has no man than this, that a man lay down his life for his friends." Sometimes we think that because we are not often asked to give our life for a friend, that kind of teaching is not for us. Jesus knew what it meant to give up something very precious for a friend — life, and other things, too. He is telling us that we show our love by sometimes giving up *whatever it is* that is precious to us, if this will help a friend. Riding a bike is not as serious a matter as giving up one's life, but a boy who thinks enough of his friend to give up his own new bike is beginning to understand something of what Jesus was talking about.

A PRAYER / *Dear God, help us to find ways to show our love for our friends. Teach us the joy of giving up something very precious to us when it helps a friend. Thank you most of all that Jesus was willing to give up his life for us so that we can know how great your love is for us. Amen.*

How Important Are Foundations?

GARY AND HIS FATHER SAT AT THE WINDOW WATCHING THE big maple trees swaying and bending in the wind. Harder and harder it blew! The sound it made was like the roaring of a great waterfall. This was the worst storm Gary had ever seen. He hoped it would soon be over.

" How do the trees keep from getting blown right over? "
Gary asked. " Look, that one is bending farther than any of
them."

" There is a good foundation under those trees," said
Father. " You think that a tree is mostly what you see standing in a field or in the forest. If you could take those maple
trees and turn them upside down, there would be just as big
a part standing in the place where the tree trunk and limbs
were. Only it would be a mass of roots instead of branches
that you would see."

" Sometimes you can see where the roots run if the earth
is not too deep over them," said Gary. " You can walk far
away from the tree and the roots keep going way out."

" That's right. They go down deep into the earth, too. The
roots grow wide and deep, just the right amount to hold up
their size of tree."

After the storm was over, Gary and his father went out
to look at the damage it had done. As they walked down the
street they saw a big truck and men working up ahead.
When they came nearer they saw that a tree across the street
had been uprooted by the wind and had been blown down.
The men were busy with their power saws cutting off limbs
and dragging them away.

" Let's go closer," said Gary. " I want to see the roots."

They walked around behind the workmen and looked at
the great pile of dirt and roots that had been pulled out of
the ground when the tree fell. " It looks bigger around
than the top of the tree," said Gary. " It must have been a
hard wind if it blew this one down."

" Now you see what I mean by a good, solid foundation
under a tree," said Father. " It's like a house. If you want
it to stand up and not be blown down by the wind and rain
storms, you have to put a good foundation under it or build
it on solid ground."

That night when Gary was going to bed, his father brought
the Bible out and opened it to Matthew 7:24-27. " Here is

something more about good foundations, Gary," said Father. " It tells about the kind of foundation a person needs if he is to be strong and stand firmly for what he believes." Then Father read Jesus' words about the man who built his house on a rock. When the rain and floods came, and the storms blew around it, the house did not tumble down. It stood firmly because it was built on a solid foundation.

Father helped Gary to understand that Jesus was telling people that the best foundation for their life was one built on his words about God's way of love. Learning to trust God and obey him is like choosing solid rock for a house foundation.

" Or like putting roots down deep, like the tree," said Gary.

Then Father gave Gary the Bible and asked him to see what Jesus said about the man who built his house on sand. You can find out what happened if you read Matthew 7:24-27 yourself. What kind of person would be like the man described in the last part of these verses?

A PRAYER / *Dear God, thank you that Jesus came to teach us the way of life that makes a good foundation for anyone who believes him. Help us to remember his words about building our life on a good, sound foundation that is like a rock, or that goes down deep like the roots of a tree. Give us the courage to stand firmly on our foundation when people make fun of us, or try to get us to go their way instead of our way. Amen.*

Hold Your Tongue!

" I CAN SWIM BETTER THAN YOU CAN," SAID TOMMY. " I'M the best swimmer in our whole cabin."

Don was new in camp, and he listened with eyes wide open. It would be great to be the best swimmer in the cabin!

"Let's go down to the lake now," said Don. "We have half an hour of swim time left. I'd like to see you swim, Tommy."

Tommy took a long time finding his swimming trunks. Then he took more time to find his towel.

"Hurry up," called Don from outside the cabin. "There won't be any time left if you don't hurry."

When the boys finally reached the lake, there was barely time for getting wet, splashing about, and a few duckings. Before Tommy had a chance to swim very far, the "All out!" whistle blew.

"You'll have to show me how well you can swim tomorrow," said Don. "Can you swim across the lake?"

"Ah . . . oh, sure!" said Tommy quickly. "Sure I can swim that far. I'm really good!"

For several days Don was in a different swimming class

than Tommy. Every time they talked about swimming, however, Tommy always had some new achievement to report. Don wished that he could swim half as well. " I'm pretty good," he said to Tommy, " but I have to work to get my endurance up. I get tired fast."

One day the camp schedule showed that the boys could have some extra free time. During rest hour Tommy whispered to Don, " How about taking out one of the canoes during free time? We're allowed if two of us go together. You ask for permission, will you? "

Don agreed. As soon as rest hour was over, Don asked the canoeing instructor for permission to take out a canoe.

" Can the fellow going with you swim across the lake? " asked the instructor. " That's our rule, you know. One man in the canoe has to be able to do that."

" Oh, yes," said Don. " He certainly can. He's the best swimmer in our cabin."

" O.K., then. But stay within the markers out there. There's a bit of a wind and the lake is likely to get choppy," said the man.

Don raced back to get Tommy. When they went to check out the canoe the older boy in charge asked, " Did you get permission from the instructor? "

" Yes, we did," said Don. " We're all clear."

Soon the two boys were paddling along through the water, out past the pier, and into the lake. " Stay inside the markers," said Don. " That's the instructions I got."

The two campers explored a little cove, tried their skill at turning, tested their speed, and were having great fun. Suddenly a brisk wind blew across the lake, sending white caps across the water. Before the boys knew what had happened, the canoe tipped and they were in the lake. The canoe got away from them, bounced along the waves, leaving the boys to swim for it.

At first they seemed to be doing well enough, but in a short time Don called to Tommy, " I'm getting tired. I'll float around here and take it easy while you go on in and get some help. But hurry up! I don't know how long I can keep this up."

At first Tommy didn't answer. Don looked across at him and saw that his face was white and he had stopped swimming, too. " What's wrong? " asked Don. " Get going, will you? I said I'm tired."

Tommy looked toward the shore. " I don't think I can make it either, Don," he said. " I can't swim that far."

Just as both boys began to panic, the canoe instructor pulled up alongside of them in another canoe. He told both of them how to get into his canoe, and when they were safely aboard he took Tommy and Don back to camp. On the way no one said a word.

After both boys were dried and dressed, the canoe instructor called them into his cabin. " Which of you boys said he could swim across the lake? " he asked sternly.

" Why, Tommy said he could," replied Don. " He said he's the best swimmer in our cabin. I told you the other fellow with me could swim that far."

" I know you did," said the instructor. " But after you started out I realized you had not told me *who* the boy was who was going with you. When I found out it was Tommy, I started after you right away. If I hadn't you both might have drowned."

Don looked at Tommy. " I thought you just got scared or something out there," said Don. " You can swim across the lake, can't you, Tommy? "

Tommy looked down at the floor. No one said a word. He knew he had to speak. " No," said Tommy in a funny kind of voice. " No, I can't."

" But you said — " began Don. The instructor stopped him.

" Tommy, your tongue talks better than you can swim," he said sternly. " You stay here with me. Don, you may go. I'll talk to you later."

That evening at vespers the leader opened his Bible and read some verses from James 3:2-8. " Look at the ships, . . . though they are great and are driven by strong winds, they are guided by a very small rudder wherever the will of the pilot directs. So the tongue is a little member and boasts of great things."

Tommy and Don did not look at each other. Can you guess what they might have been thinking? You can read the other verses for yourself, and think about some of the times when your own tongue may have caused you to be in trouble. Your tongue *is* a little part of your body, but it can cause you to say and do all sorts of things that get your whole self into good or bad acts.

A PRAYER / *Dear God, help us to remember how important our tongue is as a guide to our whole self. Forgive us when we say things that get us into trouble. Teach us to use our tongue wisely, and to keep control over it. Amen.*

New Math in the Bible!
[FORGIVENESS]

BETSY SAT AT THE TABLE WRITING NUMBERS ON A SHEET of paper, scratching them out, writing some more, and groaning from time to time. " Oh, these math problems," she said. " I'll never catch on to this! "

" What's the trouble? " asked Uncle Jack. " Are you past the two times two ones yet? "

" Don't be funny," said Betsy. " That's baby stuff. We don't do problems like *that!* "

Uncle Jack looked over Betsy's shoulder. " You're drawing pictures! " he said. " I thought you said you were studying math. What's that thing there? " and he pointed to the paper.

" That's a tub," said Betsy. " There's water coming in at

the top, and going out at the bottom, and some of it is going out here at the side. I have to figure out how long it takes to fill the tub if the water comes in faster than it can go out! "

Uncle Jack pretended to hold his head as though it hurt him badly! " Oooooh! No wonder you have a paper covered with numbers! I'd never know which end to start at."

" That's part of the problem," said Betsy. " I'm trying to remember whether to start with the top, the bottom, or the side! I'll ask Jan to come over to do these together."

That evening at the table after everyone had finished eating, Father asked Uncle Jack to read a few Bible verses for the family to talk about. As Uncle Jack turned the pages, he grinned at Betsy. " I'm looking for a math problem for you," he said.

" In the Bible! " said Betsy. " Don't tease, Uncle Jack."

" No, I'm serious," said her uncle. " Here it is, in Matthew 18:21-22. Once when Jesus was talking with his disciples, Peter asked him, ' How often shall I forgive someone who does wrong to me? Should I forgive him as many as seven

times? ' Jesus answered him, ' I do not agree with your answer. You should forgive seventy times seven times.' "

Uncle Jack paused while everyone thought about what he had said. Betsy was the first to speak up. " Did Jesus mean you should count up to 490, and forgive someone that many times? How could you keep track? "

Father laughed. " I'm glad to hear that your math is improving! But that is not what Jesus meant."

Uncle Jack shook his head. " Your father is right. It's a little like your ' tub ' problem. You have to know where to begin with this one in order to solve the problem of what Jesus meant. What had Jesus been teaching his disciples about loving their neighbor? "

The family talked about Jesus' kind of love that was for everyone, and that never came to an end. Then they talked about Jesus' teachings about loving God and our neighbor as God has loved us.

" Does God say that he will love us and forgive us just a certain number of times, and then he will not forgive us any more? " asked Uncle Jack.

" No! " said Betsy. " He will forgive us as often as we are really sorry and ask him to forgive us and help us not to do that wrong again."

" Then that's really what Jesus was saying," said Uncle Jack. " He meant that there was no certain number of times that we should forgive those who wrong us, either. The answer to this Bible math problem is not 490, but as many times as is needed! "

A PRAYER / *Dear God, help us to remember your forgiving love that is not limited to 490 or any other certain number of times. Teach us to forgive those who wrong us and ask for our forgiveness sincerely, and not to count the number of times. Thank you for Jesus, who teaches us to understand your love and to know how to live as you want us to live. Amen.*

"Now I Can See!"

MARK AND TIM ARRIVED AT THEIR CHURCH SCHOOL CLASS-room early. And were they ever glad! All around the room Mr. Martin had arranged books and pictures of cameras, telescopes, magnifying glasses, and even a big pair of binoculars. " Look around, fellows," he said. " Just be careful to keep your fingers off the lenses of the binoculars. You can take them outside for a few minutes if you like. How about planning a little report to the whole class on what you are able to see with those glasses? "

Eagerly the boys agreed, and went out to see what they

could see. When they heard the other juniors arriving, they decided that they had better go back inside.

Mr. Martin talked about some of the books and pictures, and then each junior looked at the ones he wanted to see. Then Mr. Martin asked everyone to sit down. He picked up the binoculars and said, " Mark and Tim got here a little early today, so I asked them to go outside and look through these glasses. They are going to tell you what they saw. Mark, would you like to be first? "

" Well, first we looked around just to find something to look at. We saw a bird flying up into that big tree out there. It seemed to disappear, so we looked through the glasses and we could make out the bird sitting on a branch sort of hidden behind the leaves. We could see it plainly with the glasses, but not when we looked up with only our own eyes."

" Tim, what did you see? " asked Mr. Martin.

" I looked across the valley at the mountain. From here it just looks all flat and you can't see anything on it. I looked through the glasses and I could see the trees, and there is a house about halfway up. And I could see the fire tower on the top," said Tim. " Those are great glasses! "

Mr. Martin held up the binoculars. " What are these made of? " he asked.

" There are lenses inside those black tubes, where you look into it," said Randy. " They magnify what you are looking at so you can see more than you can see with just your own eyes."

" Is there anything there when you look through the glasses that isn't there when you look without them? " asked their teacher.

" No," said Mark. " It's there. Only you can't make out the things clearly without the glasses."

Mr. Martin picked up his Bible in one hand, and held the binoculars in his other hand. " Do these two look anything alike? " he asked.

The class looked puzzled. " That's a Bible, and those are binoculars," said Tim. " They can't be alike."

" There's something alike about them or he wouldn't ask us," said Randy. " This is one of those trick questions, isn't it, Mr. Martin? "

Their teacher laughed. " It's sort of a trick," he said, " but not really. I'll ask you another. What did Tim and Mark say the glasses did for them when they looked through them? "

" It made whatever they were looking at clearer. They could see more what it was," said Randy.

" Right," said Mr. Martin. " Now, what is there in this book that could do the same thing? If you need a clue, I'm thinking especially about Jesus' teachings that we have been studying together."

" I know! " Mark said. " We talked about how he told stories instead of saying a lot of rules about what to do. The stories helped people to understand about God's love. We said the stories made things clear."

" That's what the binoculars did," said Tim. " They made the trees on the mountain come clear, and the house, and the fire tower."

" You're getting it," said Mr. Martin. " Jesus was trying to help people understand how to show in their own lives the love that God gives to us and that he wants us to show in response to him. He wanted people to look at their own lives, and see what their actions looked like. His stories and parables helped them to see more clearly their own lives as the place where they must live God's way of love. His teachings helped them to understand more clearly that way. Looking at God's love and how it can make a difference in our own lives needs better ' eyes ' than just our own understanding. It needs the kind of ' lenses ' that the Gospels give to us, to make clear the meaning of God's love for us."

Mark chuckled. " We learned that verse about ' Thy word is a lamp to my feet and a light to my path.' We could add, ' And binoculars to my mind! ' "

A PRAYER / *Dear God, thank you for Jesus, who teaches us to look always deeper and deeper into your way of love for our lives. Thank you that we never learn all that there is to know about your love. Help us to understand better how we can live as faithful and obedient people of God. Amen.*

A Log and a Speck of Dust

" MOTHER! MOTHER! " CALLED CINDY. " JAMIE'S STEALING the cookies! "

Mother looked up from her sewing. " Jamie doesn't steal, Cindy! What are you talking about? "

" He does too steal. He just stole six cookies and he took them out to give to his gang. You said we could each have *one* as soon as they were cool, and he *stole six!* " Cindy stamped her foot to make sure that Mother understood just how awful Jamie was!

" Wait just a minute," said Mother. " Jamie asked me, before I started to bake those cookies, if he could have some for his gang. I said he could take one for each boy, because I have promised to take cookies to the picnic tonight and that's all I can spare out of this batch."

" But he had one before the gang came, Mother. That's more than *one* for Jamie," said Cindy.

" Let's see, now," said Mother. " How many did you have while we were taking them off the cookie sheets, Cindy? "

" That's different," said Cindy. " Some of them were broken, and one was sort of brown on the bottom. I dropped one on the floor! And you gave me one to see if they were baked enough."

That night at bedtime, Mother said to Cindy, " I want you and Jamie to grow up to trust each other and to be kind

and thoughtful to each other. We are a family, and if you can't learn some of these things here, you may have a hard time learning them someplace else. There's a story here in the Bible that might help you to do this, Cindy."

Then Mother read the story in Matthew 7:1-5. It tells what Jesus said to his disciples once when he was talking to them about blaming or judging each other. He asked them why it was so easy for them to see the wrong that others did, but not the even bigger wrongs they did themselves. He told them that people often want to correct or bring punishment to others without doing anything at all about their own wrongdoings which may be even worse than the ones they are so eager to correct.

If you read the story yourself, you will perhaps laugh at it. Jesus said that this is like a man with a big log in his eyes that would blind him if such a thing could be, trying to point out a speck of dust in another man's eye. He said that before such a person fusses about taking out the speck in his neighbor's eye, he should get rid of the log in his own eye first!

Why do you think Cindy's mother chose that story to read to her daughter? Do you ever make a fuss about what other people are doing, when you are doing something just as wrong or even worse? Think about the log and the speck the next time you start to blame a friend or someone else for a wrong act.

A PRAYER / *Thank you, God, that Jesus sometimes makes us laugh at ourselves and at the same time makes us look honestly at what we are doing. Help us to keep the logs out of our eyes when we are being concerned about the specks in other people's eyes! Amen.*

Easter

V

EASTER IS THE MOST JOYOUS TIME OF ALL the year for Christians. The event that began with God's coming in the child Jesus at Christmas reaches its climax of fulfillment in God's coming in the risen Christ. We celebrate the sure fact that his love has not been overcome even by sin and death. God is with us forevermore! He has kept his promise. We live in the assurance of his love.

The women who visited the tomb on the first Easter morning were greeted with the words, " Do not be amazed." Yet, who is there that does not stand in wonder and amazement at what happened? Who can accept this ultimate experience of God's limitless love without feeling both the awe and the joy that combine to make the festival of Easter the most glorious celebration of the church?

Children bring to their encounter with the events of Easter many questions and much confusion. Some will have heard the story in church school and in services of worship. Many will have seen television versions of the happenings of Easter week. Still others will have only bits and pieces of information gathered from a variety of sources. Just as no two adults come to the Easter experience in the same way, so no two children ask the same questions or puzzle over the same details. It is one of the joys of Easter, however, that families can search together for the reality of the mystery that marks the difference between life and death for God's people.

Before the season is upon you, and before the children's questions begin, it would be helpful if as parents you would refresh your own memory by reading the Gospel accounts of the events of Christ's last week before the resurrection. As you read, remember that this is no story of a man being carried along by fateful circumstances. It is the affirmation of a life given to the fulfilling of God's purpose, lived in faith and trust, and firmly grounded in such complete comprehension of God's love that not even death could shake it.

It may be helpful to consider some of the kinds of questions that children ask about Easter. Even though your boy or girl may express his concerns in other ways, these will point toward some of the puzzling parts of the story. The question of death is often uppermost in children's minds at Easter. Why do people have to die? Why did Jesus die if he was a good man? Why didn't Jesus hide? In our time, many people understand something of the sacrifice of giving one's life for a great cause. Jesus' whole life was devoted to making known God's love to people. He knew that God wanted everyone to know his love that was so great it did not stop even with death. Therefore Jesus risked being laughed at, run out of town, hated, and feeling the sorrow of being rejected before he went the final road to death — all because his very reason for being was to make known God's triumphant love. Children fear separation from those whom they love and those who care for them. Jesus' death and resurrection proved once and for all that God will allow nothing to separate him from his people. Therefore, the joy of Easter brings the understanding that one need not fear death or separation.

Children need to be reminded that what Jesus taught about God's way of love was not welcome news to many people of his time. Nor is it welcome to everyone today. Jesus taught that a person who wanted to be " first " should become one who helped and served others. He taught that a person who obeyed all the laws of his religion, but treated others in unloving ways, had no right to be proud; instead, he was to be admonished and set straight as to the meaning of God's law of love. Jesus did not set himself apart from anyone who needed his help or who would listen to his message. No one was so " bad " that Jesus refused to associate with him. Thus, Jesus made many enemies. Some of them were so determined to stop his teaching and preaching that they put him to death, thinking that this would be the end of it all. Jesus knew, however, that God was with him in times of trouble and danger, and that God would be with him even though he went to his death on the cross.

Did Jesus really die — or was it like on the television programs where the " good man " appears to die, but turns up hale and hearty on the next program? Perhaps this is the deepest mystery of all, for man cannot comprehend HOW God could do this. Yet we know that ever since Jesus appeared to his friends and acquaintances following the resurrection, men have been so sure of the fact that Jesus who was dead is alive again that they have risked their lives for their belief. Because we believe in God's love and his promises, we also believe that Jesus Christ lives — although we do not understand all about it and cannot explain all that happened. It is in your own knowledge of God's continuing love and care that your faith in a living Lord is grounded. It is from this foundation that your children will sense the assurance of your faith and the sincerity of your belief.

Shouts of Praise . . . and Enemies Waiting!

[PALM SUNDAY]

CAN YOU CLOSE YOUR EYES AND SEE PICTURES OF VARIOUS places, or of people doing all sorts of things? Imagine yourself walking down a street, when suddenly you hear people shouting and singing. You look around, but at first you see nothing unusual. Then some children run by, all going in the direction from which the noise is coming.

" What's the matter? What's going on? " you ask.

" There's a king coming! Come and see him! " shouts a boy as he runs past you. " He's going to save us from our enemies! "

" You don't want to miss the king," says another. " Come on! "

Now if all this were true instead of something that you were imagining, what would you do? You would follow the crowd to see the king, wouldn't you? After all, one does not see a king every day of the week! Who would want to miss such a sight? A king must have lots of soldiers with him if he is going to save people from their enemies! What an exciting time this is!

Something like this must have taken place on the road to Jerusalem on the first Palm Sunday. There are four places in your Bible where you can read about what happened on that day. You can read the verses in Luke 19:36-40; Matthew 21:8-9; Mark 11:7-10; and John 12:12-13. You might like to take time now to read some of these verses. If you do not know who the king was, or what the people shouted, you will find out as you read.

The Sunday just before Easter is called Palm Sunday. If you go to a service of worship in your church on that day, you will find that the hymns and anthems are full of words like, " Hosanna! " " Hail to the King who comes! " " Praise him! " The minister will probably read the story of Jesus' riding into Jerusalem on a donkey, for Jesus is the King about whom the people are shouting. The reason the day is called Palm Sunday is that the people waved branches and threw them on the road for Jesus as he rode by. This was the custom at that time when a very important person rode by. Some people even threw their coats on the road.

When you hear the story, and when you hear the joyous music, you know that it must have been an exciting time. But when you count the days that came between this one when Jesus was hailed as king and the one when he was put to death, you count only one . . . two . . . three . . . four . . . five days! Have you ever wondered what happened to change the crowd from a cheering one to a mob who wanted to put Jesus to death?

You may find some answers to that question if you will put your imagination to work again. There were some people in the crowds who expected a strong and powerful king to come with a great army that would set them free from their Roman rulers. How do you think they felt about Jesus when they saw him riding into the city without any army at all? There were people who wanted to stay on good terms with the Romans and avoid trouble. How do you think they felt when they heard the crowd hailing Jesus as king, one who would be a threat to the Roman ruler? There were many people who believed that Jesus was nothing more than a good, kind teacher. How do you think they felt when the crowds hailed him as one sent by God himself? There were people who knew that Jesus had friends among the sinners and people like the publicans, who were hated by almost everyone. How do you think they felt when they saw Jesus being treated like a royal person whose ways were to be followed instead of despised? There were Romans who thought that the Jews were troublemakers who should be punished for their religious customs. How do you think they felt when the crowds around Jesus grew larger and larger?

All these people, and many others like them, must have been in the crowds that hailed Jesus as king and shouted, " Hosanna! Praise God! Here is the one who is sent from God! "

There were also people who refused to understand; people who refused to believe in Jesus; people who listened but decided that his way was too hard. There must have been many others who were puzzled, who wanted to believe in Jesus and hail him as their king, but who could not be quite sure. Yes, there were all kinds of people there that day, just as there would be if Palm Sunday were to have happened in our time.

It is hard for us to believe that Jesus' enemies on that first Palm Sunday were determined to kill him if that was the only way they could stop him from teaching and preaching about God's love. They were waiting for the time when they could do this. They were listening to the shouts of praise and wishing more than anything else that they could get rid of this troublesome man who was being treated like a king! They wanted it all to be over and done with so that people could forget that Jesus had ever lived.

A PRAYER / *Thank you, God, that some people listened to Jesus and believed in him. Help us to live in your way of love, and to shout with joy at Eastertime because Jesus was not afraid even to die to show how much you love us. Amen.*

Christ Is Risen Indeed!

HOW DO YOU GREET YOUR FRIENDS WHEN YOU SEE THEM on the way to school, or when they come to your door and want you to play? Do you say " Hi! " or " Hey, Robbie "? What do you say when something very important or exciting has happened to you?

In the long-ago time when the church was very young, Christians greeted each other in a special way to show that something important and exciting had happened to them. One would greet a friend by saying, " Christ is risen! " The reply was, " Christ is risen indeed! "

The words are simple ones, but what they meant was the most important thing in all the world to the Christians. People risked their lives on the truth of these few words. No matter what might happen to them, as long as they were sure that Jesus Christ, God's own Son, was not dead, but was alive . . . everything was all right! God was still the ruler of his world. His plan would never be defeated.

Say the words yourself, " Christ is risen! Christ is risen, indeed! " Many people greet each other with these same words at Eastertime today. Maybe you have sung them in church, or maybe you have spoken them. We mean just what the early Christians meant by them, for we gather at Eastertime to worship God and celebrate our praise and thanksgiving to him for Jesus Christ, who shows us that God's love is more powerful than even death.

Have you ever wished that you could talk to some of the people who lived in Jesus' time? You could ask them questions about the amazing events of the first Easter, and they could tell you what they saw and how they felt. But would you be surprised to know that even they, who were right there, could not explain to you *how* it was that Jesus was dead, and then was alive again. They could not tell you *why* everything happened as it did. They might even be impatient with you for asking so many *how* and *why* questions! The important thing for them was that they *knew* that Jesus had been put to death rather than deny God's love and power, because they had been there and seen the terrible scene. But they also *knew* that Jesus was alive, because he had been with his friends — eating and talking with them. They could not explain all the why's and how's, but they were sure Jesus was alive and with them as he had promised. Jesus had never lied; he had never broken a promise. He was alive and with his friends, just as he had said!

When you go to church on Easter, think about the friends of Jesus. Think how they must have felt when they thought that they would never see him again because he had been put to death. Then think how they felt when he came to them, spoke to them, and ate with them! " Chist is risen! " said one follower to another with great excitement. " Christ is risen indeed! " was the answer.

These friends could hardly wait to tell the good news to others. They did not say, " I *think* that Jesus is risen! " or " I hope my eyes are not playing tricks on me! " They were sure — and they were full of joy.

There is a word that helps to explain how we, too, can believe that Jesus is alive. That word is " faith." We trust God's promises because he has always been faithful. We believe that Jesus came to make known God's love to us. We grow in our understanding that at Easter, God's love proved itself stronger than even death.

A PRAYER / *Dear God, we thank you for the mystery of Eastertime. We thank you that we cannot understand everything that happened at the first Easter, for your love and your power are greater than anything we can imagine or think of. We thank you that Jesus' friends have told us about their feelings when they knew that he was alive and with them, just as he had promised. We thank you that men have risked their lives for your way of love because they know that Jesus lives, and nothing can defeat your plan for men to love each other. Help us to know that Jesus lives and is with us today, just as he promised his friends many years ago. Amen.*

Prove It!

HOW MANY THINGS DO YOU BELIEVE ARE TRUE, BUT YET you cannot prove? Has anyone ever made you say, " Well, I can't prove it, but I know it's true "?

Tomorrow you may go out the door of your house or apartment on your way to school. You may go down the same streets, cross at the same corners, and there the school building will be — right where it was yesterday and the day before and ever since it was built. How did you know when you left home this morning that it would be there? Could you see it with a magic eye? Did you ask someone if it would be there? You just *knew* it would be there, didn't you?

Tonight you may go to bed after the stars and moon are

out. You know that when you wake up at your usual time the sun will be shining, or the clouds may be hiding its brightness. How do you know that the sun will be up? Do you ever wonder whether or not it will be shining when you awake? How do you know that day will follow night?

If you had magic eyes so that you could see inside your body, you could watch your heart beating and see your blood being pushed through hundreds of veins and arteries. How do you know that someday, all of a sudden, your blood will not start to flow backward? Can you prove that it will never get all mixed up and try to go two ways at once?

If the winter is cold and the summer is hot where you live, how do you know that when summer comes you will not need your snow boots and heavy coat? Why do you pack your bathing suit instead of your warmest clothes when you go to summer camp? Can you prove that the weather will be warm in summer and cold in winter?

What do you answer when someone asks, " Do your

mother and father love you? " or " Do you love your parents? " Can you show them a basketful of love that they can measure? Do they give you love in a box or bag that you can carry around with you?

Maybe some of these ideas sound silly to you! After all, you can *see* your school building. If you were a scientist, you could explain why night follows day, and why seasons change. Your doctor can draw you a picture to show why blood flows the way it does. You can tell the ways by which your parents show their love for you. Even so, can you really *prove* these things to someone else unless he tries it or sees it work for himself? " Try it, and then you'll see " is often the only proof you can offer.

Sometimes this is the best answer the church has for people who want someone to prove that what Christians believe about Jesus and God is really true. " Prove it to me, and then I'll believe," they say. The best answer you can give may be, " Try it for yourself, and then you'll see! "

This is one of the important reasons for celebrating Easter. We not only sing " Christ is risen! " and say that Jesus is alive. We also remember that people ever since the first Easter have trusted God's promises and lived their lives in the faith that all Jesus taught and showed us about God's love is true. In our Bible we read of God's acts of love and faithfulness to his people, and there is never one story about God breaking his promise. We read Jesus' teachings and learn how he lived, and we find that he trusted God so much that he was not even afraid to give his life because he was so sure of the greatness of God's love. We know about Christians who had the courage to face persecution and death because they believed that Jesus would always be with them — and he was. The Christian faith is not easy to *prove* — in fact, you can't prove it at all unless you try it!

Read Acts 2:1-8 and 43-47 in your Bible to find out what happened to the disciples who were waiting for Jesus' Spirit to come to them as he had promised. What do you suppose might have happened instead if these men had insisted on knowing all the answers about *how* God's power could come in this way, and whether they could be *sure* it would work before they went out to preach and teach?

How do you know that a car will work unless you drive it? How do you know that directions for making a model will work unless you try them? How do you know that a camping trip can be fun unless you go on one? How do you know that God's love will make a difference in the way you live your life unless you trust him and accept his love? Can you think of any other way to *prove* it?

A PRAYER / *Thank you, dear God, that Jesus was not afraid to trust your love even as far as death. Help us to understand that this same love is for us, and that it will give us courage and help us if we try it. Teach us more about your way of love, so that it is your love and not our own ideas about it that we trust. Amen.*

Was It for Real?

RICKY TURNED OFF THE TELEVISION AND SAT DOWN ON THE floor. He thought and he thought — and then he thought some more. He thought about the program he had just seen, the one that told about what happened to Jesus on Good Friday and on Easter.

That night at bedtime Ricky asked his father, " Jesus didn't really die, did he, Daddy? It was like in the television show . . . after it was all over and everyone had gone away, he just got up and started looking for his friends, didn't he? He didn't really die! "

Father sat down on Ricky's bed. " I'm afraid you have it all wrong, Son," he said. " Jesus did really die. All the sad part about the way people treated him, and finally killed him, is true. It is not at all like the television show."

" But why, Daddy? Jesus was the best person there ever was! It's not right that he should get killed," said Ricky. " And anyway, you always say that he is alive! Did he die, for real? "

Father was quiet for a minute. " You ask good questions, Ricky — and hard ones to answer. But I'll give it a try. First, though, I have to tell you that I do not have all the answers. No one does. If anyone did, I guess he would know as much as God himself . . . and that's not the way of things. Let me ask you this: What are some of the stories you know about Jesus? "

"Well," said Ricky, "I know about when he was born, and growing up and learning to be a carpenter, and about the disciples' going with him when he helped people, and all that."

"Right," said Father. "You know he is a real person, don't you? Jesus is not just someone in a story. He really lived, and worked, and did all the things real people do. He felt happy and sad, and he was troubled when people would not love God, who loves them so much."

"U'mmmmm," said Ricky. "But everyone didn't like him. Some people said he disobeyed the laws because he took care of people on the Sabbath Day when the law said not to do any work."

"Right again," said Father. "But did Jesus stop doing what he knew was right just because it made some people dislike him?"

"Oh, no," said Ricky. "He didn't try to hide, either. Remember when he got Zacchaeus down out of the tree so that he could go home and eat with him?" Ricky chuckled as he thought about the little man who had climbed up into the tree so that he could see Jesus going by. And then, he ended up having Jesus as his guest! Who ever thought that Jesus would want to eat with a man like Zacchaeus, whom everyone said was a cheater?

"Then we know that Jesus kept on doing God's work, even though he made some enemies," said Father. "When he came before the rulers on Good Friday, Jesus knew perfectly well why some people hated him and wanted to get rid of him. He could have said that he had made a mistake, and that he was just a poor teacher who wanted to help people . . . and he would have had a good chance of going free. But why was Jesus here at all, Ricky?"

Ricky looked puzzled. "Well, God sent him. He wanted Jesus to teach us what God is like . . . how much he loves us, and all that."

"Now we're getting to the real answer to your question,"

said Father. " Jesus came to do the work God sent him to do. If God wanted him to teach us that his love is the most powerful force in the whole world, Jesus had to be willing to put that love to the hardest test. If God's love is stronger than death, Jesus couldn't just *pretend* to die in order to make people believe this, could he? "

" They would say he cheated! " said Ricky. " They might say that the other things he did were tricks, and that what he said was just a lot of lies. People wouldn't know for sure whether they could believe in him or not! "

" I think you have answered your own question," said Father. " It's hard to believe, I know. Even Jesus' best friends had trouble believing that such a wonderful thing could be true. Tomorrow I'll read you a story about a time when Jesus met some friends who walked along talking to him . . . and at first they didn't even know who he was! Good night now, Ricky. Sleep tight! "

(The story Ricky's father read to him is in your Bible in Luke 24:13-35. Ask someone to help you read it. Remember that these events happened on Easter, just after the men had learned from their friends that Jesus was alive. Think how you might have felt if you had been in their place!)

A PRAYER / *Thank you, God, for keeping your promise that your love is greater than anything else in the world. Help us to trust you always, and to live in the way of love that Jesus teaches us. Thank you that Jesus was not cheating on the first Easter Day. Thank you that he trusted your love to be stronger than the wrong that men can do. Amen.*

VI

WE DO OUR CHILDREN A GREAT DISSERVICE when we do not share with them stories about the men and women who have responded to God's claim upon their life in circumstances that are more than usually dramatic or exciting. Great figures in history, in science, in any field — including religion — communicate something of their devotion and courage when we read and hear about their exploits. All too often boys and girls think of the " heroes of the faith " as people who obeyed God so easily and wholeheartedly that they experienced none of the problems with which other people struggle. Therefore, they are removed from our life as surely as are the make-believe heroes whose daring thrills us without challenging us.

Children often learn as much from human failures as they do from " success " stories. The Bible tells of countless characters who had to learn to accept God's forgiveness and believe that he could use even their fumbling ways. The history of the church is filled with the stories of those who dared to stand firm in their belief in Jesus Christ, and whose lives ended in seemingly useless disaster. There are men and women working and witnessing to the faith throughout the world today whose courage and daring is as great as that of any current hero you can name. Living as a Christian has always been a dangerous business!

In the following pages, you will find a few stories of " heroes of the faith " whose lives may speak to the needs of your children. There are examples of those who made difficult decisions, those who struggled to stand by their choices, those who dared to stand alone, and those who were sure their lives were failures. You will find many other such stories to share with your children if you watch for them in books, magazines, newspapers, and elsewhere. Maybe someone in your own family should be recognized as such a hero!

People with a Mind to Work

THE KING OF PERSIA WAS A RICH AND POWERFUL RULER.
Among his most trusted servants was a man named Nehemiah, a Hebrew. One day, as Nehemiah was bringing in the
great golden cup, the king noticed that his servant looked
very sad.

" What troubles you, Nehemiah? " he asked.

Nehemiah sighed as he spoke. " O King, my city of Jerusalem is in ruins. Its walls have great holes through which
the enemy can enter to attack my people. While they live
there, helpless to protect themselves, I live here in your fine
palace where I need fear no one! "

The king agreed to allow Nehemiah to return to Jerusalem to see if he could help to rebuild the city walls. He gave
his servant a letter ordering the keeper of the forests to provide wood that Nehemiah would need for the job. He even
gave him horsemen and army officers to protect him on the
long journey.

When the travelers came in sight of the city, Nehemiah
could hardly believe what he saw with his own eyes. The
holes in the wall were bigger than he had imagined. The
gates were in ruins. The people were ragged and hungry,
and they looked at this stranger suspiciously. Why would he
be coming to their city, dressed in his fine clothes and surrounded by an armed guard?

Nehemiah must have wondered, too! He must have wished
to be back in the comfortable court of the king who trusted
him and treated him well. He may even have been a little
frightened at the angry looks and unfriendly treatment he
was receiving in Jerusalem. Maybe he wished that he had
never taken on the job of rebuilding the city walls.

At first Nehemiah talked to no one. He had work to do,
and he set about it. First he had his servants prepare him a
place to live. Then he was ready to inspect the walls. One

night, when the moon was shining brightly on the piles of tumbledown stones, Nehemiah and a few of his men started off to look closely at what was to be done. They stumbled around in the stones, kicked at the charred wood left from the burned gates, and made their plans. Then they returned to the city as quietly as they had left it.

Finally Nehemiah was ready to begin work. He called the people together and told them his plan. " Jerusalem is in ruins. The city can never be protected as long as it is in this condition. Come, let us rebuld the wall and repair the gates so that we can protect ourselves and be proud of our city once again! "

The people just stared at each other! " Does he think we don't know there are holes in the wall? " they asked. " What does he expect us to repair them with? And what will the king think, and the people living around us, if it looks as though we are trying to fortify our city? "

Then Nehemiah showed them the king's orders. He told how the king had promised to help by providing the wood and sending Nehemiah to help with the work.

" Let us rise up and build! " shouted the people.

" Yes, let us rise up and build," answered Nehemiah. " Listen and I will tell you my plan."

When every man had been given a job, and when the special parts of the work had been assigned to trained workmen, the building began. Slowly the walls rose higher and higher, strong and well built. Even the threats of the people from outside the city could not stop the work. Some men stood guard while others worked. Every person in the city took his turn doing something to help.

In fifty-two days the wall was finished. No enemy would dare to attack the city now. The people could live in Jerusalem in safety. They could be proud of their work, and they wanted to give thanks to God. " We have worked with the help of God," they said. " Let the leaders tell us how to keep the thanksgiving feast. We have lived for so long in a

strange land that we have forgotten."

Nehemiah ordered the people to come together in the month of harvesttime. He asked one of the leaders to read aloud from the Law. When the people heard the words, they were sad. " We have not been faithful to God," they cried. " We have not kept his laws."

Then Nehemiah spoke. " Do not be sad. Let us gather food for the hungry. Let us all rejoice that God is our strength. He has helped us in this time of trouble. Let us rejoice."

The people gathered to praise God. They promised once again that they would serve him and love him forever. They would try to be his faithful people. " Surely the joy of the Lord is our strength," they sang.

A PRAYER / *Dear God, we give thanks that men like Nehemiah have led your people in their times of trouble. Help us to learn from their courage and hard work that following your way is not always easy, but that you never leave us to do the job alone. Help us to be faithful in the work we are asked to do. Teach us to trust in your strength and to be joyful that we are your people. Amen.*

A Bishop and a Bandit

LONG, LONG AGO A GROUP OF CHURCH LEADERS SAT WAIT-ing for their beloved bishop to come to visit in their town. Suddenly a young man came running into the room and announced breathlessly, " He's coming! The bishop is coming! "

Quickly the leaders arose and crowded to the door to welcome the guest. He was an old man, with a flowing beard and with eyes that sparkled as he looked around at the group. " Peace be with you," he said gently. " God's peace be upon this church."

The church leaders told the bishop about their problems, and about the many new members who had joined the fellowship of Christians. The bishop gave the leaders good advice, and told them to be careful to instruct all the new followers in the way of love as Jesus taught. Then he asked about the young man who had been the one to tell the others of his arrival.

" He is one of the newest of those who have asked to join our fellowship," said one of the men. " He is a fine fellow, and I am sure he will be a faithful follower."

The bishop liked the young man and found several occasions for talking with him about being a follower of Jesus. When it was time to leave, the bishop asked the church leaders to give special attention to the young man so that he too might become one of the leaders. " I will expect to find him among you when I come again," said the bishop. " Take special care of him, for I love him like my own son."

Months passed, and once again it was time for the bishop

to visit the same group of church leaders. One of the first things he asked them was, " Where is my young son whom I left in your special care? "

The church leaders looked at one another. No one wanted to tell the bishop what had happened! Finally one of them said, " Dear sir, it makes us sad to have to tell you that your son has become a bandit. He lives out in the hills with a band of robbers. We never see him; we only hear about his doings from those who have been robbed by his men. He is known as one of the most fierce of all the bandits in the area. He is lost to the church."

At first the bishop would not believe their story. " A fine young man like that could never become a robber! Surely I could not have been so wrong about him. I will go and see for myself! "

The church leaders tried to persuade the bishop not to risk his life for such an evil young man. " He would not listen to us," they said. " If you go out into the hills, his men may kill you. He chose this life for himself. Why not just let him alone? Your life is too precious to risk trying to bring him back into the church."

The bishop paid no attention. He set off for the hills, and after some time found the robber band. He commanded them to take him to their leader. The two men stood face-to-face, the kindly old bishop and the cruel young bandit. The bishop spoke quietly, begging the young man to give up his evil life and return with him. " You are so important to me that I have risked my life to come out here after you," said the bishop. " Come back with me, and spend your life following Jesus' way of love instead of this dishonest way of robbing innocent people."

The young man was so amazed that the bishop loved him so much that he *did* return to the church. He became a faithful follower of Jesus Christ, and served the church well. The story of the bishop's courage was told again and again, and became an example to all those who needed to be reminded that *every* person is important to God and worth any risk in bringing him into the fellowship of those who love God.

This story is a legend told by a famous historian of long ago. The bishop is the famous early church leader, John, whose well-known words make a good rule for us today: " My children, love one another."

A PRAYER / *Dear Father, teach us to love one another. Give us the kind of courage that John and the early followers had, so that we may be faithful followers in our time and in the ways that we find in our daily life. Amen.*

In the Name of Christ, Stop!

AN OLD MAN WAS WALKING SLOWLY ALONG THE DUSTY road leading to the great city of Rome. His name was Telemachus, and all his life he had dreamed about making this trip. Now he was almost there! Far ahead he could almost make out the shapes of the buildings.

As Telemachus came closer to Rome, the road became crowded with people all hurrying away from the city! " Where can they be going? " the old man wondered. " Why are they hurrying from the city? "

Just then one of the men passing by shouted at him, " Hey there, old man! You're going the wrong way. This way to the fight! Hurry or you'll miss it! "

So that was it! If everyone else was going, Telemachus decided that he would go too, and he turned to follow the crowd.

Inside what looked like a big playing field, he found a place to sit high up in the rows of seats that circled the field. The crowd began to shout as two men came out and faced each other, ready to fight. Suddenly Telemachus realized that those two men were not just going to fight — they were going to kill each other! And he would be sitting there watching!

The old man never stopped to think. He jumped to his feet, waved his arms, and called out as loudly as he could, " Stop! In the name of Christ, stop! "

At first no one paid any attention. Telemachus kept on shouting, and when no one would listen he walked right down to the field and tried to step between the two fighters.

"Get away, old man," shouted one fighter. "I'll kill *you* instead if you don't get back and let us fight."

The old man refused to move. "You must not kill each other," he said. "I tell you to stop, in the name of Christ!"

The crowd laughed and jeered, but Telemachus would not move. Finally the fighters became so angry that one of them stepped forward and ran his spear through the old man's body. Telemachus sank to the ground. He was dead.

No one knows what happened after that. History books tell us of such an action that brought an end to fights in which one man had to die before the fight was declared ended. The old man who risked his life never knew that because of his courage in refusing to sit by and watch one man kill another, this cruel kind of entertainment would come to an end. He was only one man who did what he believed was right.

A PRAYER / *Dear God, when the time comes for us to show bravery and to stand up for what we know is right, give us courage enough for the task. Help us to make decisions about right and wrong that are pleasing to you. Help us to try to show that we believe in your way of love. Amen.*

A Dangerous Book

Do you know that there was a time when you and all your family would have been sent to prison — or even put to death — if you had been caught reading the Bible? Do you know that a copy of the Bible once cost about two hundred dollars? Do you know that people often gave a whole load of hay in payment for sharing a neighbor's copy of a few pages of the Bible?

All these things happened at the time when a man named John Wycliffe was telling people that if they wanted answers to their questions about God and his command, they should

go to the Bible and find them there. That sounds easy enough, doesn't it? But the Bibles were written in Latin, and most of the people could not read them. What then was the use in going to the Bible?

John Wycliffe asked some of his friends to help him translate the Bible into the English language. That sounds easy too, doesn't it? Except that in the first place there were no printing presses, so that every copy had to be written by hand! (How long does it take you to copy *one page* of an assignment for school?) And in the second place, the church leaders did not want everyone to read the Bible and make up his own mind about what it meant. That might lead to dangerous disagreement with the church's thinking, and the leaders would have none of that!

John Wycliffe sent out men who were known as the " poor priests " to carry the Bible to the people in the little towns and villages. Wherever they could find one or two, or a group of people who wanted to hear the Scripture read to them, the " poor priests " would stop and read. All they asked for was a bit of food and a place to sleep in return for their work. All over England, people heard the words of the Bible in language they could understand. Then they wanted to hear more, and still more. They learned parts of the Bible by heart and recited them for each other. They borrowed copies from anyone who had enough money to buy a Bible. They traded pages with each other when they had only enough money to buy part of a Bible.

But all this had to be done in secret! For the church leaders of that time did not approve of this Bible-reading. They arrested those caught with a Bible in their possession, and burned some people for reading it. They burned all the copies they could get their hands on. They tried every way they could think of to stop people from reading God's word for themselves.

Of course their schemes failed. God intends that his people shall know and understand his word. There were brave men like John Wycliffe who risked their lives to bring the Scriptures into people's homes. Because of him, and others just as brave, you and I can walk into any bookstore or library, pick up a copy of the Bible, and read it as much as we wish.

The next time you open your Bible, think about the long-ago days when it was a dangerous book to own or to read! You are reading the Bible today because men were willing to risk their lives to make it an " open book " for everyone.

Why not read a familiar psalm like Psalm 23 and try to say it from memory. Pretend that you are in danger of having your Bible taken away from you! How much of it could you remember and share with someone else?

A PRAYER / *For the Bible, with its good news about your great love, we give you thanks, O God. For men who risked their lives so that we can read it in safety, we give you thanks, O God. Teach us to value it, and obey its teachings, so that we may grow to be faithful followers of your way of love, O God. Amen.*

Filled with Spirit!

[PENTECOST]

DAVID WAS RIDING HIS BIKE ALONG THE STREET, WONDER-ing where he should go and what he should do for some fun on this warm, spring Sunday afternoon. It felt like the kind of day for doing something special!

Suddenly he heard music! David took off for the big field around the corner from his house, where the sound seemed to be coming from. There he found a crowd of people laughing and talking. He saw gaily-colored posters on the sides of the buildings along the field. He heard a band play-ing and some boys singing. It looked and sounded like a carnival!

This looks like fun, thought David as he leaned his bike against a wall and snapped the safety lock. People walked by him, talking in Spanish and English and some languages he didn't understand. I wonder who they are, he puzzled.

He stopped to read one of the posters and had a little trouble with the words. PENTECOST FESTIVAL were the words he saw printed in big, black letters.

Just then David saw one of the older boys from his church. " Hi, Stan! " he called. " What's going on here? "

Stan ran up, carrying a bright orange-colored costume on one arm. " Hi! Some fun, isn't it? It's the festival, don't you remember? "

David frowned. " I sort of remember . . . but not re-ally. What are we celebrating? "

Just as Stan started to explain, a voice over the loud-speaker called, " Gather around, everyone. It's time for the service. Everybody is welcome."

The two boys squeezed into the front row and sat down on the grass. When nearly everyone on the field had come close enough to hear the speaker, the man on the platform motioned for quiet. " We have come here today to celebrate

one of the greatest days in our church," he said. " It is like the church's birthday, and we want to make it as happy as any birthday can be! In case you are wondering why we have planned this noisy festival instead of a quiet time of worship together, I will tell you. When we began to make our plans, we thought about the time when the disciples were waiting in the upper room in Jerusalem for the strength and power Jesus had promised would come to them. We re-

membered how frightened they were, and how they puzzled about how they could go out to teach and preach God's love. Then we remembered that on the day we now call Pentecost, God's Spirit came upon the men, making them so excited and joyous that they rushed out of the room, unable to keep quiet about the good news that Jesus lives and that God's love is stronger than anything else in the world. Shout it, tell it, sing it! Everyone must hear! That sounded like a festival to us, and that's why we are celebrating Pentecost today with the same joy and excitement. Because those men received power to go out and preach, the good news has come to all men — to you and to me."

" Now you remember, don't you? " Stan said.

David nodded. But the man on the platform was speaking again. " I am going to read from the Bible the story of the event we are celebrating. Then we will sing a hymn praising God for his love and power." Following this, another man prayed a prayer of thanks to God for the church, asking him to help all the people to be faithful followers of Jesus and to help them tell the good news of God's love in every way they could.

That evening David told his family all about the festival. He told about the groups that danced and sang, and about the big mural that anyone who wanted to could work on to show what he thought the church was all about. He told about the cookies and cakes and hot dogs to eat. He told how the speaker said at the end of the afternoon that people filled with the spirit of the church did not need to be sad and quiet — they should be joyous and excited about the good news, just as the men were long ago when they knew they could go out to teach and to preach.

" I wish the disciples could have been here today," said David. " Maybe they would think it was funny to see us eating hot dogs! But I guess they would have been happy to see so many people filled with so much spirit! "

(You can read the story of Pentecost in Acts 2:1-13.)

A PRAYER / *Thank you, God, for sending your Spirit and power to the men long ago at Pentecost. Thank you for your Spirit, who fills people with joy and courage to tell the good news today. Thank you that church people can get excited and be happy about your great love. Amen.*

Under a Haystack . . . But Not Fast Asleep!

DO YOU REMEMBER THE NURSERY RHYME ABOUT LITTLE Boy Blue who was sent out to tend the cows and the sheep, but who was found under a haystack fast asleep instead? The sheep got into the meadow where they were not supposed to go! And the cows trampled down the farmer's corn! Everyone was cross with Little Boy Blue who went to sleep under the haystack.

Once upon a time some college boys were under a haystack . . . but not fast asleep! They were friends who had gone for a walk in the fields on a mountainside. The sun was hot and they were tired, so they stretched out under some trees and began to talk. They talked about another friend who had gone far away to China, where he was preaching and teaching about God's love.

" Think of all the places in the world where there are no preachers! " said one boy.

" There must be millions of people who will never hear one word about Jesus and his way of love," said another.

" Why don't we go and tell them? " asked a third boy. " We could study and become ministers! Then we could go."

The boys became so excited that they hardly noticed the black clouds gathering in the sky. The wind began to blow, and raindrops fell on their faces before they realized that they were caught in a storm. " Make for that haystack! "

shouted one fellow, and they ran for shelter just as the rain began to pour down.

While they waited for the storm to pass, the boys could not talk about anything else but the idea of going to faraway places to preach the gospel. They promised each other that they would spend their lives in this work, and they prayed to God for help in showing them the way. After they got home, they wrote to some ministers to tell about their plan and to ask for help. Finally the men became ministers themselves, and all but one of them did go far away to become missionaries.

Who would ever think that getting caught in a rainstorm and having to take shelter under a haystack would have anything to do with deciding what to do with your life? Little Boy Blue went to sleep! But because some other boys wanted to do God's work, they did not sleep under their haystack! They planned and prayed and went out to prepare themselves for whatever God intended them to do.

(This incident is based on the story of how students from Williams College decided to become foreign missionaries in the Far East. You sometimes hear their conversation under the haystack called " The Haystack Prayer Meeting.")

A PRAYER / *Dear God, help us to be ready to talk and to think about your plan for our lives. Help us to keep our minds awake to what you want us to learn, and to what you expect us to do. Amen.*

Miss Tooter!

MARIE AND JAN SLOSHED ALONG THE WET STREET TRYING to keep their books from getting soaked as the wind whipped the cold rain across the lake. " Let's stop at the drugstore for a hot chocolate," said Jan. " I'm cold. I hate this weather."

" Can't," muttered Marie. " We signed up for this tutoring thing at the church and the kids are waiting for us. They got out of school earlier than we did. Come on, walk faster! "

" Ugh! " said Jan. " I wish I hadn't! Those kids probably don't want to learn to read any more than I want to teach them! "

The two girls walked on, thinking about the day when the idea that they could help in an afterschool project seemed like such a great one! Boys and girls in the neighborhood who could not read needed help, or they might get so far behind in school they would drop out.

" We're always talking about helping other people," Jan had said. " Here's our chance. Let's sign up."

" I will if you will," Marie had agreed. " Let's not just talk."

But now the work was to begin, and neither girl really wanted to give up time for the project. Nevertheless, they had promised and they would not go back on their word. They arrived at the church, pushed open the heavy door, and went inside. A sign in the hallway said STUDY ROOM and an arrow pointed toward a big room in the basement. Jan and Marie followed the arrow and soon were in a room that seemed to be full of noisy boys and girls.

Before long the lady in charge of the project had led Jan and Marie to a table and introduced them to a boy and a girl each about ten years old. " This is John and this is Carmella," she said. " And these two girls are your tutors — Miss Jan and Miss Marie." Then she left them to carry out the plan she had explained the week before when all the tutors met for their instructions.

Jan and Marie tried to get the children to talk about themselves. But John and Carmella could do nothing but giggle. What could be so funny? Finally Jan said sternly, " You must stop giggling! We are here to help you read! What is so funny about that? "

John looked at Carmella, who was almost sober-faced by this time. " Toot! Toot! " he said. And the children laughed so hard they almost fell off their chairs.

Marie suddenly began to laugh with them. " I get it! " she said. " They think we are ' tooters ' instead of tutors! Maybe they're waiting for us to blow a horn! "

Jan laughed, too. " Right here is where we begin the reading lesson," she said. " Tutor and tooter! No wonder they laughed! "

From that day on, both Jan and Marie were called " Miss Tooter " by the children. Weeks later, when they listened to John and Carmella reading aloud as well as any ten-year-

old, they thought back to that first day when they came to the church expecting to hate every minute of their work. " I wouldn't have missed this for anything! " said Jan. " I've signed up for next semester already."

" So have I," said Marie. " I want to try tutoring in math next time."

" You mean ' tooting ' in math! " laughed Jan.

Not many people can be great heroes because of their faith, or go to faraway lands to preach and teach, or do anything special that will make everyone remember them forever. Most people are like Jan and Marie — like you and me and your family and friends! There are decisions we must make about how we will respond to God's call to us to show our love toward others; decisions about whether or not to work or just talk; decisions about whether we will treat people as God intends or as though they do not matter. When we do our best to make these decisions wisely, and stick to our good choices, we are heroes in God's sight. He knows how hard it is to give up time to help others. He knows that we do not always feel loving toward others. He knows we need his help. And he knows that the way we feel about ourselves when we know we have been faithful to him will be a surprising kind of payment that comes when we least expect it!

A PRAYER / *Dear God, we confess that we do not always want to help others, or take time to show love toward them. Help us to remember your gift of love to us in Jesus Christ. Teach us to make wise decisions and stick to them. Help us when we want to turn away from following your way of love. Thank you for your forgiveness and love. Amen.*

Special Occasions

VII

No ONE CAN TELL WHEN THERE WILL OC–ccur in a family special occasions or events that call for " something to say to the children " that will help them to understand or accept what is happening. Often these happenings are related to sorrow or trouble. But sometimes they are especially happy occasions that call for a celebration. Whichever they are, parents are wise to remember that God's help is for both extremities of our lives.

The following readings may help you to recognize some of the kinds of situations when a word about God and his promises to us is needed, and must be pertinent to the occasion. Some of these may be useful to you. Others will serve only to suggest ways of approaching the matter of special days and unusual experiences in your life together as a family.

A Birthday

JIM WOKE UP, STRETCHED HIS LEGS UNDER THE BLANKETS, and looked out at the bright sunshine. At first he had to *try* to think about what was so special about this day, for he wasn't quite awake yet! But all of a sudden he *was* awake! " It's my birthday! " he said aloud. " Today's my birthday! "

Jim jumped out of bed, raced to the bathroom to wash, and back to his room. He pulled off his pajama top, and started to pull his undershirt on over his head. It wouldn't come! He pulled and tugged, and pulled some more. But his arms just stuck up like a scarecrow's, and he could not get them through the place where arms should go. He looked down and saw another undershirt lying on his bed. Quickly he shook off the first shirt and pulled on the other. It went on just the way an undershirt should!

Jim continued to dress, but a funny thing happened. The first of every piece of clothing he tried to put on just would not fit! It was too small! What was going on here?

Even Jim's shoes were too small — the first pair, that is! Right beside them was another pair — the ones he had taken off last night, he was sure of that!

Jim ran down the stairs and into the kitchen for breakfast. "Happy birthday, dear," said Mother.

Just as Jim started to tell about the terrible time he had trying to get dressed, he looked down at the table. There where he usually sat were two plates, two glasses, two sets of silverware. One was the kind he always used, and the other was small and looked like baby dishes! On each plate was a small box, wrapped in bright colored paper, tied with ribbon, and holding a card that said " JIM."

Mother pretended to be very busy at the stove cooking the eggs. But Jim knew that she was watching out of the corner of her eye, and she was smiling her sort-of-secret smile! He decided to open the box on the baby plate first — maybe it was a trick! Carefully he unwrapped the box, took off the lid, and unwrapped another package that he found inside.

" Oh, Mother! " he shrieked. There in the wrappings was the first little wristwatch he had received when he was five years old! It had hands that moved, a tick-tick-tick that sounded when you wound it, and a picture of a cowboy in the middle of the watch face. It looked like a " real " watch! And it was what he had wanted more than anything else — on his fifth birthday.

Quickly, but very carefully, Jim unwrapped the second box. There he found another wristwatch . . . but this was a " real " one. It was exactly like his big brother Bob's, and one that had a second hand and wouldn't stop if you happened to forget to take it off when you went swimming! It was exactly what he wanted more than anything else on this birthday!

Mother began to laugh, and Jim laughed too. " You did all that business with the clothes! " he said. " You put out all those little ones that I couldn't get into, Mother. Why did you do that? "

" Birthdays are great days, Jim," she said. " Daddy and I tried to think of some way to remind you that this birthday marks a new step you have taken in growing up. We decided that this would do it! "

" It did," said Jim. " That's for sure! "

When Father came down to breakfast, everyone had another good laugh. Jim showed his parents, and then his big brother Bob, how he had tried to get into his " little-boy clothes."

Then Father asked Jim to think about some other ways he had grown up, too — like being able to walk to school alone, knowing what to do when he forgot to take his lunch, remembering that baby Susan depended upon him to look after her when Mother left him alone to watch her, and understanding a little better why a boy had to be honest and trustworthy. (Can you think of some other ways Jim might have named?)

Father turned to a verse in the Bible and asked Jim to read it. " ' Stop and consider the wondrous works of God,' " read Jim.

" You are one of the most wondrous of those wondrous works," said Father. " That's why Mother and I played this trick to make you stop and think! Growing up is one of God's best gifts to his children, and we should take time to think about it once in a while. A birthday is the best time I know for doing that! "

A PRAYER / *Dear God, thank you for birthdays. Thank you that we grow in many ways — some that we can see and some that we can feel. Thank you that we can grow in ways of thinking and acting toward ourselves and others. Thank you for the special love that people show us on this day, for presents, and cards, and birthday cakes, and all the fun we have. Help us to remember that growing up makes people expect more of us. Thank you that you expect more of us, too, and that you will help us to grow to be the person you know we can be. Amen.*

Give Us Courage, O God
[AN ACCIDENT OR TROUBLE]

MOTHER KNEW THAT SOMETHING WAS WRONG THE MINUTE Betsy came home from school. Something was very, very wrong because Betsy was crying her honest-to-goodness cry, not just her I-feel-sad-today one. Mother turned off the vacuum cleaner and put both arms around her. " What's wrong, dear? What happened? Are you sick? "

Betsy shook her head. " Mickey's hurt," she sobbed. " He's hurt a lot. A big truck hit him over at the corner. They took him to the hospital. He couldn't move his legs. Oh, Mother, why do such awful things happen to people? "

Mother didn't answer for a moment. She just held Betsy

close and hugged her hard. Then Mother said, " Before we start trying to answer questions, let's ask God to take good care of Mickey right now at the hospital."

Betsy blew her nose and tried not to start crying all over again.

" Dear God, please help the doctors to make wise decisions about taking care of Mickey. Help them to use all their skill and all the right medicine so that he will have whatever he needs most. Keep Mickey in your loving care in a special way, and help him to know that your love is there to give him strength and courage. Show us how to tell Mickey that we love him and want to help him. Heal Mickey's hurts in the way you know is best. Thank you that we can come to talk to you about our hurts and sadness. Thank you for your great love. Give us courage, O God. Amen."

Betsy and her mother were quiet for a long time. Then Betsy said, " One day we made up prayers in church school, and someone said, ' Give us courage, O God,' was a good prayer. But I wish Mickey didn't have to be having courage. I wish he wasn't hurt at all."

" I know, dear," said Mother. " I guess everyone prays for strength and courage, and at the same time would like not to have to need any extra for times like this. It's hard to explain. Sometimes we think we would like to wave a magic wand, and make everything harmful in the world disappear. But we can't fix everything to suit ourselves, and we can't stop all accidents from happening. Even when we make good safety laws and teach our children to be careful, people are hurt by cars and trucks as well as helped by them, no matter how hard we work at this. We just have to keep trying. And we need to pray for courage, knowing that at one time or another we are going to need it."

" Does it really work, Mother? " asked Betsy. " Does God really give us courage? "

" Yes, he does," said Mother firmly. " That's one thing I am sure about. He does not make everything come out all

right, and he doesn't ask us to pretend to *like* the pain and
the sadness that come to us, but he does help us to do something about it. We must remember always how he has kept
all his promises to his people, and one promise was that he
would always be with us to hear us when we come to him.
When we stop thinking only about the bad part and try to
figure out what to do to help, something happens that begins to make us feel different. You see, you have to be willing to *accept* the courage the way God gives it. Right now
we must find out whether Mickey's mother needs someone
to take care of the other children while she goes to stay with
Mickey at the hospital."

" And I'll take his books back to the library," said Betsy.
" He was going there after school because they are due to-

day. Nobody else will remember. When can we start sending him cards and stuff, like I got when I had my tonsils out? "

" I'll find out as much as I can, Betsy. Then we'll make some plans right away," said Mother.

" I think I feel some courage coming, Mother. I hope Mickey does, too," said Betsy as she went to wash off the marks of the tears. " I'll go and get Mickey's books right now."

A PRAYER / *Dear God, we need courage just now in a special way. Help us to remember that you have promised to be with us always, and to help us when we are in trouble.* [Pray specifically for the one who is ill or injured or in trouble, asking God to guide those who are responsible for caring for the person about whom you are praying.] *Thank you, God, that we can trust your love to hold us and keep us from giving up hope. Amen.*

(Some verses to read in times of special trouble are found in Psalm 56:3-4, 9-11.)

Who Are You?
[FOR A CHILD WHO FEELS INSECURE]

" I'M JUDY DAVID AND I HAVE MORE NEW DRESSES THAN anyone else in my grade at school."

" I'm Danny Marvis and I can run faster than anyone else in our whole block."

" I'm Peter Kelley and sometimes I don't have enough to eat."

" I'm Pedro Continez and my family just moved here from South America."

Who are YOU?

Try to answer this question by putting your own name in here when you say, " I'm _____." If you wanted to, you could end by saying, " _____ and I'm one of the most important people in the whole world! " That would be exactly right — and you would not be bragging, either! Do you know why?

We often say that God made all people. But we do not stop to think just how important it is that he made each one of us different from every other person. He made you special in your very own way. There is not another human being anywhere else on earth who is exactly like YOU. God made everyone in your family a special person, too, but each in his own way. Each one of us is a very important person to God.

This must mean that God has something in mind for each one of his people, or that he expects us to act in special ways toward these persons of his whom we know and meet. This is part of the secret of what it means to be Christian. God intends that you be HIS VERY IMPORTANT person, loving him and acting toward others as you believe is a right and good way to show your love for God.

Maybe this does not sound very important or special to you! But stop to think what kind of family yours would be if each of you could really show this love for each other — or what kind of town or community you would be living in if everyone in it followed Jesus' way of love — or even what a different world we might have if everyone in it really tried to show love toward others.

This special kind of home or town or world has to start somewhere. In fact, it has already started — with God and his Son Jesus Christ, who shows us and teaches us how to live in the way of love. But it cannot go on without people like you and me who are willing to live as Jesus teaches. You may say, " I'm only one! I don't count! " But the wonderful thing about God's plan is that he can take all the " ones " and make something of them, something wonderful and great, because this is what he wants of each of us.

There is a short verse in I John 4:19 that you could learn to say from memory if you do not know it already. " We love him, because he first loved us." You could think of these words today wherever you are. Perhaps they will help you to remember to show love to someone even when it is hard, or when you do not feel at all like doing it. Remember that you are one of God's special people to whom he has shown his love so that you can show love to others.

(Some other verses to read are I John 4:7-12, 19-21.)

A PRAYER / *Dear God, thank you for making us all special people with special work to do for you. Thank you for showing your love to us by giving us your gift of your Son Jesus Christ. Thank you that we can show our love to you by acting in loving and forgiving and thoughtful ways toward the people we will see today. Help us to do this even when it may be very hard to do. Amen.*

The Best Book of All

[ON RECEIVING ONE'S FIRST BIBLE]

DID YOU KNOW THAT THERE ONCE WAS A TIME WHEN Bibles were as rare as the most precious jewels? that one copy of the Bible was more expensive than anything money could buy? Those were the days before a printing press had been invented. That was the time when each Bible had to be copied carefully and with much effort during long hours of work. The monks wrote each word by hand, checking each line to be sure they had not made a mistake. They tried to make their finished product so beautiful that everyone who read it would know how much the writer loved the book that he had copied.

If you ever go to a great museum, you may be able to see one of these ancient handwritten Bibles — or at least a page from one. Long, long ago the most important books were written on a kind of paper called vellum that had been dyed purple, the color that always reminded people of kings and royalty. A few copies of the Gospels (the first four books of the New Testament) written on this purple paper have been kept from as long ago as the sixth century! If you stop to think that you live in the century called the twentieth, you can count back and figure out how many hundreds of years ago these books were written. It is a VERY long time ago!

The writers who copied the Bible so carefully were not satisfied just to use purple vellum. They wanted to find other ways of showing how wonderful and precious the Bible is, so they began to decorate some of the capital letters at the beginning of some of the sentences. Sometimes they traced beautiful designs and decorations around the letters. Sometimes they painted them with silver or gold. Sometimes they decorated and then added bright colors to make their work even more beautiful. We call this " illuminating " the letters.

If you would like to see how much time and work it took to do this, take your crayons or paints and try to make a large capital letter look just as gay and beautiful as you can. You might even copy a short Bible verse on a piece of cardboard and try to decorate the first letter of the first word. You would then be " illuminating " a letter!

No one was paying the monks who copied and decorated the Bibles. No one had hired them and offered to pay large sums of money for the best job. They were simply men who knew that the word of God was the most important thing in all the world. Anything they could do to make his word known to people everywhere was worth their best time and effort, no matter how long it took or how tiresome the copying became. The Bible is the greatest book in the world, and they wanted to make it look so!

Pick up your Bible. Turn its pages. Look for one or two of your favorite verses. Think about the men who copied it long ago by hand so that there would always be Bibles in which men could read about God's faithful promises, his mighty acts, and his great love. All this happened so that you could hold your Bible in your hands today. God intends that his people shall know his word. Are you ready to use your Bible as though you, too, believe that it is the most important book in the world?

Read a favorite passage today, or turn to Psalm 23.

A PRAYER / *Thank you, God, for the people who lived long, long ago and who copied the words of the Bible carefully so that none of them would be lost and we could read of your love for us. Help us to remember that the Bible is helpful to us when we read it and study it. Teach us to understand its words, to ponder over its teachings, and to follow your way of love as we learn of it from the life and teachings of Jesus. Amen.*

Beth's New Home

[MOVING TO A NEW CITY]

BETH WATCHED THE BIG BLUE MOVING VAN BACK CAREfully out of the driveway and start down the street. She watched until it was out of sight, away down at the end of the street. It was a nice enough street, but it didn't look at all like the one Beth had lived on out in California.

Beth hugged her Sally doll close. " I wish we were at home," said Beth. " I *do* wish we were at home instead of here."

" Who's making wishes? " asked Father as he came around the corner of the house and gave Beth a hug. " Let's have some lemonade. What color cup do you want, Bethy? "

" Where's the lemonade? The refrigerator isn't working yet. I'll have a green cup, please," said Beth.

" Yes, ma'am," said Father. " Step right this way for lemonade in a green cup! " Father took Beth's hand and up the front steps they went. Inside in the hallway there was a big pitcher, some pretty paper cups, and a box of cookies.

Soon everyone was drinking the cool lemonade and munching on the cookies. " They are from Mrs. King, our neighbor next door," said Mother.

" She doesn't know us yet," said Beth.

" Well, not exactly," said Mother. " But we're neighbors, she knows that! She is going to be a good neighbor."

Just then one of the men from the office where Beth's father would be working knocked at the door. " Hello," he said. " My wife, Margy, wants you all to come over and eat a picnic in our backyard. Don't bother to change your clothes. I know how much work there is to getting settled in a new house. Come on over any time you want to, and we'll eat when you get there."

Beth watched him go down the walk and get into his car. " How do we know where to go? " she asked. " How did he know we were here? "

Father explained that his company had told the office people when he would be arriving and when he would start to work. " I met Mr. Clayton, the man who was here, at a meeting not long ago. When he knew we would be moving into this neighborhood, he said he would keep his eye out for us. I guess he did! "

The next day another neighbor from across the street came over to meet the new family. " Won't you bring Beth over to splash in our wading pool," she said. " It is right there in the corner of the yard, and you can look across the street and see your house all the time you are playing."

Just across the street wasn't far! Soon Beth was splashing and shouting with Kathy and Ricky, just as though they were friends! Why, they *were* friends! She stayed for a sandwich and chocolate milk, and promised to walk to school with Kathy in a week or so when school opened.

That evening Father said, " We are all going to take time off from fixing up our house. We are going to find out where to get a bus, where to get on the subway, and where some of the stores are."

The next day the family did just that. Before very long they began to get " the feel of the place," as Father put it. " Cities and towns are sort of like people. You have to get to know them before you can decide whether you like them. I like this one."

" I like this one, too," said Beth. " There's a zoo we can go to someday. The man in the ticket booth said it wasn't far away."

" I have some leaflets that tell about all sorts of places to go and things to see," said Mother. " We will take them home and decide which ones we want to see and then we can plan some trips. I want to get acquainted with my new city, too."

That night Beth was tired so she climbed into bed early. The curtains were not up at her windows. The toys were not

all on the shelves. But she had Sally doll, and Mother and Father were here, and she had new friends, and she was getting acquainted with her city — it was beginning to feel like home!

(Here is a verse that Beth might have read to remind her that God does not forget about his people, either, when they move from one place to another: " The Lord will keep your going out and your coming in from this time forth and for evermore." You will find it in Psalm 121:8.)

A PRAYER / *Thank you, dear God, that you never leave us, even when we move from one place to another. Thank you that we are never lost from you. Thank you for good neighbors, and for loving parents, who show us love and who take care of us even when we are in new and strange places. Thank you for interesting places to go and new things to see. Thank you, God, for your love. Amen.*

New Baby!
[A NEW CHILD IN THE FAMILY]

BILLY LOOKED AT THE FUNNY LITTLE RED-FACED BABY lying in the big basket that was all full of soft blankets. " Is *that* my new brother? " he asked. " Why doesn't he look at me? I'm his big brother."

Daddy and Mother both put their arms around Billy and gave him a special " double hug." " Oooomph! " he grunted. " You're squashing me."

Daddy looked at the baby. " He's asleep, Billy. But even when he wakes up, it will be a while before he will want to look at anything except something to eat! He won't be able to see who you are until he grows up a little more. Then he'll be proud as proud can be to know that *you* are his big brother. He's a lucky baby! "

" Did I ever look like that? " asked Billy.

" You certainly did," said Mother. " Bring me the book of snapshots from the shelf over there, and I'll show you how you looked the day you came home from the hospital. I hunted for it just before I left to have Baby John."

Billy looked at the picture his mother showed him. " Did you love me when I looked like that? " he asked. " I looked funny! "

Father sat down and Billy climbed up on his lap. " Big brother Bill," said Father, " we loved you then —all red and wrinkled up. We love you now — all strong and good-looking. We love Baby John just the way he is right now, and we love you just the way you are right now."

"Do I get half as much love now?" asked Billy. "There are two instead of one."

Mother smiled. "That's the best thing about love, Billy," she said. "There's no end to it. You don't have to divide it up, a bit here and a bit there, trying to make it come out even. It's like going to a barrel and always finding it full and running over! No matter how much you use, there's always more than enough left. That's the way our love for you is."

Father rumpled Billy's hair. "Now that you're the big brother, I guess we will have to treat you like an older boy. I think there had better be a bigger allowance for you. And we can count on you to take a turn at looking after Baby John. It's great having a helper around that we can trust."

"I think I'll buy Baby John a present," said Billy. "I'll buy him a little baseball. I'll keep it for him till he gets big enough to throw it. Then I'll teach him how."

"Let's go out and have a game of catch," said Father.
"We'll have to keep you in practice so you'll be ready for
Baby John when he's big enough to play."

A PRAYER / [This is the prayer Billy's father prayed that
night when Billy went to bed.] *Dear God, thank you for our
son Billy. Thank you for making him part of our family.
Thank you for our new Baby John. Help us to make him welcome, and care for him in our family. Teach us to love each
other in your way of love. Thank you for sending Jesus to
teach us and show us that there is never an end to how much
love people have for each other, because God's love is always
more than enough for us all. Amen.*

(You might like to use the verse in II Corinthians 12:9,
in this form: "My love is enough for you.")

All Those Eyes!

[FIRST DAY OF SCHOOL]

MIKE HELD TIGHTLY TO DADDY'S HAND AS THEY WALKED
down the street. He held tightly as they climbed the steps of
the big school building. He kept holding tightly when Daddy
found room 6 and Miss Rose said, "Good morning, Mike. I
remember you. My name is Miss Rose. Come in and I will
find a friend for you."

Mike couldn't remember just how it happened, but suddenly he was not holding tightly to Daddy's hand. Instead,
he was holding some big wooden blocks and trying to decide
how to build a garage with them!

The next thing Mike remembered was that he got hungry!
It was time for lunch! His stomach said so! Soon he was sitting at a table in the lunchroom. He looked at the food on
the plate in front of him. He looked at all the boys and girls
around him. It seemed as if they were all looking at him! He

couldn't eat with all those eyes staring at him.

Just then Miss Rose sat down beside him. "That's the best peanut butter and jelly sandwich I have ever eaten," she said as she finished the last bite of her lunch. "You'll like it, Mike." She started to talk about the garage he had been building upstairs in the first-grade room, and before he knew it Mike had finished his sandwich and his carrots and his milk and a chocolate cookie! Things happened fast at school!

That afternoon Mike got tired. He was ready to go when Mother came to walk home with him. " Good-by, Mike," said Miss Rose. " I'll see you tomorrow. I have a surprise that I think you'll like."

Mike turned back. " What is it? " he asked.

" It's a secret surprise," laughed Miss Rose. " You will find it first thing in the morning when you come into our room. Good-by."

Mike didn't hold tightly to Mother's hand on the way home. He even forgot he was tired. He was wondering what the secret surprise would be in his room when he went to school tomorrow!

That night Daddy tucked Mike into bed. " It's part of God's plan for boys that they go to school and learn many things so that they can grow up and be happy boys and happy men. It's part of his plan that people learn to use their hands and their heads the very best way they can. It's part of God's plan that mothers and fathers show their love by helping their children go to school and learn many things."

Mike went to sleep thinking about how great it was that God's plan had a secret surprise like the one Miss Rose had promised him tomorrow!

A PRAYER / *Thank you, God, for schools where we can learn to use our minds and our hands and our bodies. Thank you that it is part of your plan for boys and girls to grow up, and learn to be useful and happy people. Thank you for teachers and for schools. Help us to work hard and have lots of fun. Thank you, God, that going to school has secret surprises! Amen.*

Some Prayers and Graces

Thank you, God, for a happy day,
　For food and friends,
　For work and play. Amen.

For this new day
　　And all it will bring,
　We thank you, dear God,
　　For everything. Amen.

Now before we go to play,
　We bow our heads and pause to pray:
Thank you, God, for love and care,
　For all your goodness everywhere. Amen.

God is great, God is good.
　Let us thank him for this food.
By his gifts we all are fed.
　　Thank you, God, for daily bread. Amen.

Thank you, God, that we can sleep
　Safe within your loving care.
Thank you, God, for watching close
　O'er little children everywhere. Amen.

For parents, home, and friends to love,
　Thank you, God our Father.
For work and play and time to rest,
　Thank you, God our Father. Amen.

Supplementary Books

ABOUT GOD'S WORLD

Barlowe, Sy, *A Child's Book of Stars*. Maxton Publishing Corporation, 1953.

Barnett, Lincoln, and the Editorial Staff of *Life,* ed. by Jane Werner Watson, *The World We Live In*. Golden Press, Inc., 1956.

Bendick, Jeanne, *All Around You*. McGraw-Hill Book Company, Inc., 1951.

Blough, Glenn O., *Who Lives in This House?* McGraw-Hill Book Company, Inc., 1957.

Brown, Margaret Wise, *A Child's Good Night Book*. William R. Scott, Inc., 1943.

Elmo, Horace T., *The Golden Picture Book of Questions and Answers*. Simon and Shuster, 1957.

Fisher, James, *The Wonderful World*. Garden City Books, 1954.

——— *The Wonderful World of the Sea*. Doubleday & Company, Inc., 1957.

Harper & Row, leaflet series, *The Basic Science Education Series: Water Appears and Disappears; The Sky Above Us; Clouds, Rain, and Snow; Flowers, Fruits, Seeds; Insects and Their Ways*.

Hogben, Lancelot T., *The Wonderful World of Communication*. Doubleday & Company, Inc., 1959.

Lewellen, John, *The True Book of Moon, Sun and Stars*. Children's Press, Inc., 1954.

Marino, Dorothy, *Goodbye, Thunderstorm*. J. B. Lippincott Company, 1958.

Memling, Carl, *What's In the Dark?* Abelard-Schuman, Ltd., 1954.

Muller, Carolyn Edna, *God Planned It That Way*. Abingdon Press, 1952.

Simon, Norma, *The Wet World*. J. B. Lippincott Company, 1954.

Walters, Marguerite, *See How It Grows*. Wonder Books, Grosset & Dunlap, Inc., 1954.

Wolcott, Carolyn Muller, *God Gave Us Seasons*. Abingdon Press, 1958.

ABOUT JESUS AND HIS TIMES

Chalmers, Muriel, *Jesus, Friend of Little Children*. Thomas Nelson & Sons, 1947. See also *When Jesus Was a Boy*.

Kunhardt, Dorothy, *Once There Was a Little Boy*. The Viking Press, 1946.

Lloyd, Mary Edna, *Jesus, the Children's Friend*. Abingdon Press, 1955.

————— *Jesus, the Little New Baby*. Abingdon Press, 1951.

Rubin, Alvan D., *A Picture Dictionary of Jewish Life*. Behrman House, Inc., 1956.

Smither, Ethel Lisle, *Early Old Testament Stories*. Abingdon Press, 1954.

————— *First to Be Called Christians*. Abingdon Press, 1955.

————— *A Picture Book of Palestine*. Abingdon Press, 1947.

Tubby, Ruth, *A Picture Dictionary of the Bible*. Abingdon Press, 1949.

Wernecke, Herbert Henry, *Christmas Songs and Their Stories*. The Westminster Press, 1957.

ATLASES

Kraeling, Emil G. (ed.), *Rand McNally Historical Atlas of the Holy Land*. Rand McNally & Company, 1959.

Rowley, H. H., *Modern Reader's Bible Atlas*. Association Press, 1961.

Terrien, Samuel (ed.), *The Golden Bible Atlas*. Golden Press, Inc., 1951.

Wright, G. E., and Filson, F. V. (eds.), *The Westminster Historical Atlas to the Bible*. rev. ed. The Westminster Press, 1956.

BIBLES

The Holy Bible. Revised Standard Version. Thomas Nelson & Sons. 1952.

The New English Bible: New Testament. Oxford University Press and Cambridge University Press. 1961.

The New Testament in Modern English. Translated by J. B. Phillips. The Macmillan Company. 1958.

Bible Readings for Boys and Girls. Thomas Nelson & Sons. 1959.